F. G. PACI

ESSAYS ON HIS WORKS

EDITED BY JOSEPH PIVATO

GUERNICA

TORONTO·BUFFALO·CHICAGO·LANCASTER (U.K.)

2003

Joseph Pivato, Guest Editor
Guernica Editions Inc.
P.O. Box 117, Station P, Toronto (ON), Canada M5S 2S6
2250 Military Road, Tonawanda, N.Y. 14150-6000 U.S.A.

Distributors:
University of Toronto Press Distribution,
5201 Dufferin Street, Toronto, (ON), Canada M3H 5T8
Gazelle Book Services, Falcon House, Queen Square,
Lancaster LA1 1RN U.K.
Independent Publishers Group,
814 N. Franklin Street, Chicago, Il. 60610 U.S.A.

First edition.
Typesetting by Selina.
Printed in Canada.

Legal Deposit — Fourth Quarter
National Library of Canada
Library of Congress Catalog Card Number: 2002114652
National Library of Canada Cataloguing in Publication
F. G. Paci : essays on his works / edited by Joseph Pivato
(Writers series ; 12)
ISBN 1-55071-177-6
1. Paci, F. G. – Criticism and interpretation.
I. Pivato, Joseph. II. Series: Writers series (Toronto, Ont.) ; 12.
PS8581.A24Z65 2002   C813'.54   C2002-905352-8
PR9199.3.P274Z65 2002

CONTENTS

ACKNOWLEDGEMENTS

The editor would like to thank the following people for making this volume possible:the contributors for producing the original essays to support this project; the author, Frank Paci for co-operating with many helpful details, and Emma Pivato for proofreading.

We thank the authors and Guernica Editions for permission to use Marino Tuzi's essay from *The Power of Allegiances* (1997) and Roberta Sciff-Zamaro's excerpt from *Contrasts* (1985).

I would also like to show my gratitude to Antonio D'Alfonso for supporting this project as part of the Writers Series and to the many editors from across Canada who have made this series of volumes such a general success. Each book is an act of love in support of a Canadian writer and of Canadian culture.

I dedicate this volume to my own black madonna, the late Mary Pivato née Sabucco.

INVISIBLE NOVELIST

An Introduction

JOSEPH PIVATO

Frank Paci is Canada's invisible novelist. Since 1978 he has published eight novels but we hear or read little about him. In 1982 his *Black Madonna* was one of the first feminist novels to deal with ethnic minority women, and is still studied in university and college courses. His first novel, *The Italians* became a Canadian best-seller by 1979 and was later translated into French as *La famille Gaetano*. He has a series of novels set in Toronto, but nobody in that city has heard of him. Even writing under the name, F.G. Paci, has helped to maintain his anonymity. Is this the shyness of the immigrant child who feels awkward in the new country and has a sense of difference which will never allow him to fit into the new society? Or is it the negative capability of the artist who thinks of his vocation with religious austerity?

In an era of instant celebrities and shameless self-promotion Frank Paci shuns publicity and avoids even small literary readings and conferences. Paci believes that the writer should focus on his craft and not on media images. While he welcomes literary reviews of his books and academic criticism of his narratives, he sincerely maintains that the work should speak for itself.

The essays collected in this volume deal with some of Paci's eight novels and explore several literary themes, moral questions and philosophical preoccupations of this little-known author. We do not pretend that these essays will make Paci famous, but we do hope that they contribute to a better understanding of his literary works and an appreciation of his achievements.

Frank Paci has been called one of the fathers of Italian-Canadian writing. His book, *The Italians*, was the first English novel to deal with the experience of Italian immigrants in Canada. Since 1978 Paci has chronicled this experience in powerful realistic narratives which have inspired other writers. In Quebec Marco Micone produced the play, *Gens du silence* (1979) "voiceless people" which could have served as the symbol and title of Paci's early novels.

There are now about one hundred writers of Italian origin publishing across Canada. Most work in English, some in French or Italian, and thus demonstrate the diversity of this group of writers. They are scattered across the landscape from Anna Foschi and Genni Gunn in Vancouver, Caterina Edwards in Edmonton, Peter Oliva in Calgary, to Giovanni Costa in Quebec City. As a result of Paci's publications and the work of other writers, Italian-Canadians are no longer the voiceless people. At an early stage Paci recognized his social role as an artistic voice for his community, for the forgotten generation of his parents, for the immigrant women who are seen and never heard.

In an interview with Dino Minni in 1985 Paci articulated the social aspects of his vocation as a writer. "There is a need to preserve the accomplishments of my parents, with the accent on 'serve.' I had the voice they didn't have. It's this very sense of preserving that acts as a catharsis, because as you're writing the story of your parents you're also coming to terms with your background and defining yourself in a historical context" (6). It is a vocation in the full sense of the word. A life dedicated to the sacred task of writing. In his series of novels which begins with *Black Blood*, Paci speaks of the writing vocation in terms of a religious ritual of black blood.

There is a revealing scene in his novel, *Sex and Character*, in which the protagonist, Mark, meets Margaret Laurence during her term at the University of Toronto as Writer-in-Residence. The scene is based on Paci's own meetings with Laurence in Toronto and is probably the closest that he has come to writing autobiography. Mark is an aspiring writer and Laurence is giving him advice on his manuscript for a novel. She asks him, "Why didn't you write about your background . . . you know, your family and roots . . . ?"(164).

It is evident that Paci has followed this advice and has written about his Italian immigrant background and the people of Sault Ste. Marie. In a sense he is not a Toronto writer like Morley Callaghan because he is not writing about people established in the familiar urban scene, but about exiles from Northern Ontario and from Italy. Toronto is not home for these people. And in this sense he is writing in the tradition of Margaret Laurence since there is always a home somewhere else in the background.

Unknown Characters

In 1983 Paci was invited to Edmonton to give a reading with the senior Alberta novelist, Henry Kreisel. The host was Athabasca University, the audience was large and mixed and Paci was nervous. Kreisel was on stage first, and gave a dramatic reading of his famous short story, "The Almost Meeting," that left us spellbound. Paci was not satisfied with his reading. I recall this event because that story, "The Almost Meeting," was ironically symbolic of the encounter itself: the young writer travels across the country to meet the senior writer he has admired only to fail to have a meeting of two minds. Such are the difficulties of the tasks of the writer devoted to his or her art. Many questions must remain unanswered.

The search for the answers to the mysteries of life is a life-long adventure with many failures along the way. These enigmas are the main focus of each novel by Frank Paci. The most memorable mystery is the Black Madonna herself, the widowed mother Assunta, whom nobody seems to understand. There is also Oreste Mancuso, the baker in *The Father*, who remains largely unknown to his friends and family. In *Black Blood* Mark's friend Perry dies young and before anyone can get to know him. Later in the big city Mark encounters people, Patrick Murphy, Halina, and Amanda, whom he spends years trying to understand.

The essays collected here look at specific novels by Frank Paci and examine the mysteries that he tries to explore. In 1985 one of the first studies on Paci's writing was Roberta Sciff Zamaro's "*Black Madonna*: A Search for the Great Mother," which delved into the enigma of this woman character and suggested the larger mystery to which she was connected. We have a short excerpt from that essay here.

A number contributions to this collection try to deal with the unanswered questions of Paci's characters by comparing them to personalities in other novels. Enoch Padolsky traces many parallels between *Black Madonna* and Margaret Atwood's *Lady Oracle*, an appropriate title. Gaetano Rando explores the father figure in *The Italians* and in *The Sensualist* by Italian-Australian novelist Antonio Casella. Alberta novelist, Caterina Edwards examines the plain style in the development of character in *Black Blood* and *Under the Bridge*. Religious iconography is the focus of Anna Carlevaris as she reads *Sex and Character* in the context of Paci's other novels.

Not included in this collection is "Hating the Self: John Marlyn and Frank Paci," an essay which compares Sandor Hunyadi in Marlyn's Winnipeg novel, *Under the Ribs of Death*, to Lorianna and Bill in *The*

Italians. I wrote this essay before the appearance of *Black Madonna,* a novel which portrays the most graphic and powerful image of ethnic self-hatred to be found in North American literature. And any essay on ethnic self-esteem is incomplete without a reading of *Black Madonna.* Maybe it is for this reason that this novel is still studied closely by students: there are elements in Marie's lack of self-esteem that many of us can either identify with or understand at a deep level.

By looking beyond the question of self-hatred, Marino Tuzi explores the whole issue of identity formation in *Black Madonna* in the context of theories of irony, narration and symbolism. What he finds is that the Italian-Canadian identity is marked by the contradiction of continuity and transitoriness. On these questions Paci anticipates the narratives of Dino Minni, Caterina Edwards and Nino Ricci.

Return to Italy

In 1991 Paci began the *Bildungsroman* of young Mark Trecroci with *Black Blood.*

With the fifth novel in this series, *Italian Shoes* (2002), Paci takes Mark Trecroci back to Italy for the necessary pilgrimage of self-discovery in the old country of his parents and ancestors. Will this be the key event in his life which will help Mark find his true voice and turn him into a successful writer? We know that many other Italian-Canadian writers have used their first return trip to Italy as a stimulus for their writing (Pivato, 1985). Pier Giorgio Di Cicco identifies this watershed event in the Preface of *Roman Candles* (1978):

> In 1974 I returned to Italy for the first time in twenty-odd years. I went biased against a legacy that made growing up in North America a difficult but not impossible chore (or so I thought). I went out of curiosity and came back to Canada conscious of the fact that I'd been a man without a country for most of my life. (1)

In a 1984 interview Mary di Michele explains the significance of the return trip in terms of her dual identity and her poetry:

> I made only one trip in 1972. I spend the summer there with my whole family . . . My Italian identity started to come out more and more. By the end of the summer I started to dream in Italian. (21)

In his interview with Dino Minni in 1985 Frank Paci spoke of his first Italian trip in 1972 and confirmed that "this trip was the catalyst that finally made me see that I had to come to terms with my Italian background before I could write about anything else"(6).

In the first chapter Mark Trecroci recalls the words of advice from Margaret Laurence to write about his Italian background: "You have to write from the heart, kiddo." As he is writing in his travel journal and talking to his aunts and uncles Mark begins to see his parents in a new light. He rediscovers the Italian father he lost to emigration. He begins to feel close to this alienated man lost in the back-breaking labour of the steel plant in Sault Ste. Marie. He sees that his parents had left behind not just their brothers and sisters and extended families, but a whole social context of towns and villages, a whole cultural context of Italian language, food and music. In contrast to the act of emigration his aunt and uncle take him to the cemetery and demonstrate that even the family dead are always with them, that there is an eternal pattern here in this rocky soil. The Mark of *Black Blood* who doubted his own identity could not imagine this family history.

In *Italian Shoes* we find an Italy of simple country people, of sensuous foods, strong smells, bright sunshine and rolling green hills. Nostalgia is everywhere. Mark must visit his relatives on both sides of the family and his father's old friends. He is there to represent his parents and to be witness to the changes that have taken place since their year of emigration. The war, poverty and hardships are often recalled. There are few young people like himself since many have left the villages to work in the big cities. The time is the 1970s and the economic miracle will soon change Italy forever. Mark sees this Italy from the point of view of the returning immigrant rather than the tourist.

Later Mark meets up with Amanda, his girlfriend, and their friends, as they travel from Venice to Florence. They visit many art galleries in both cities. They stop at his uncle's farm and spend some time helping with the grape harvest. Here they encounter the other Italy of the poor peasant and realize the contrast to the Italy of cities, high art and museums. In Rome they are young tourists who become saturated with churches and museums. The four friends argue and fight.

Mark visits the ancient Roman catacombs to find yet another Italy, that of the eternal spirit. By the time that Mark boards his plain for the flight back to Canada he has undergone a change and has made a new friend, Lisa James. In *Sex and Character* Mark and his student friends were seeking a mature spirituality; by the end of *Italian Shoes* he is on that road. Did it take his experiences in Italy to make Mark a more mature person? Do aspiring writers need to travel to Europe? It is a postcolonial dilemma.

Frank Paci has consistently made references throughout his novels to the great philosophers of Europe. For the most part they tend to be rationalist philosophers rather than moralists or mystics. In *Italian Shoes* Mark constantly quotes Wittgenstein, and Plotinus. However there is a mystical quality which emerges as Mark encounters work after work by the great artists of Italy. We cannot understand the life force behind these extraordinary people. It is a spirituality which transcends time and the material limitations of the immigrant. This aspiring writer is learning about the meaning of art and of life. Europe is a centre in Paci's imagination, and yet there is also the northern landscape of Canada. As Lorenzo says in *The Italians*,

This is the only thing I like about the new country – the
space, the giant of a space. Out here no-one bothers you.
It's too big . . . There is land everywhere . . . my parents
they would faint if they saw it. (17)

The History

In Halifax in 1981 when I delivered the first conference paper on Italian-Canadian writing I began with
references to Di Cicco's *Roman Candles* and Paci's
The Italians (Pivato, 1982). This novel identified
many of the problems in Italian families and the
themes in ethnic minority writing. Frank Paci has
always been part of the history of Italian-Canadian
writing as his novels have followed the development
of the Italian communities in Canada. In *The Father*
Oreste Mancuso is concerned about the value of his
work and the respect of his family. Marie Barone
rejects her Italian identity and her mother only to later
discover her loss. Mark Trecroci begins a long quest
for his authentic voice as a writer and must travel
many miles to find it.

The work of Frank Paci is inseparable from the
development of Italian-Canadian writing. And he
shares many characteristics with the other fiction
writers like Dino Minni, Caterina Edwards, Marisa
De Franceschi, Nino Ricci, Peter Oliva and Maria
Ardizzi. They have all had to balance the powerful
pull of Italian cultures, both the peasant culture of
Italians in North America and the high culture of
Italy, with the popular cultures of North America.

Paci captures this phenomenon in sensuous detail in his short story, "Growing Up With the Movies."

The young Mark goes regularly to the movies to see his favorite Hollywood actors play the strong, silent heroes typical of films from the 1940s and 1950s. He begins to strongly identify with these men who idealistically did their duty and won the girl in the end. When Mark's mother takes him to see Italian-language films he finds that men and women behaved differently. The dutiful hero does not win the girl. She does not remain faithful to him, but goes off with the weak, foppish character. The young Mark who is just beginning to develop his own identity and sexuality becomes shocked and confused with these different values and attitudes towards personal loyalty and women. Why did these Italian films portray such a negative view of heroism and of the loyalty of women? Why did these Italian films question the values and ideals depicted in American films? The Italian immigrant characters in the stories of Dino Minni and Caterina Edwards are often confused by these different values and behaviours between Italy and Canada.

Frank Paci has spent a life time exploring these differences and writing about us, Canadians with diverse cultural backgrounds. His novels are testaments of this devotion to the art of fiction and the reality of life. It is very ironic that this "father of Italian-Canadian literature" is also an invisible novelist.

WORKS CITED

Di Michele, Mary. "Immigrant Daughter and Female Writer," *Vice Versa*, I, 5-6 (1984).

Di Cicco, Pier Giorgio. "Preface," *Roman Candles*. Toronto: Hounslow Press, 1978.

Kreisel, Henry. *The Almost Meeting and other stories*. Edmonton: NeWest Press, 1981.

Paci, F.G. "Interview" with C.D. Minni, *Canadian Literature* 106 (1985).

_____. *Sex and Character*. Ottawa: Oberon Press, 1993.

_____. "Growing Up with the Movies," in *The Anthology of Italian-Canadian Writing*. Ed. J. Pivato. Toronto: Guernica Editions, 1998.

_____. *Italian Shoes*. Toronto: Guernica Editions, 2002.

Pivato, Joseph. " The Arrival of Italian-Canadian Writing," *Canadian Ethnic Studies* XVI, 1 (1982).

_____. "The Return Journey in Italian-Canadian Writing," *Canadian Literature* 106 (1985).

Sciff Zamaro, Roberta. "*Black Madonna*: *A Search of the Great Mother*," in *Contrasts*. Ed. J. Pivato. Montreal: Guernica Editions, 1985.

THE CONFESSIONS OF MARK TRECROCI

Style in Frank Paci's Black Blood *and* Under the Bridge

CATERINA EDWARDS

> Oh, those words that came into me, filling my body
> with the heady elixir of black blood.
>
> *Under the Bridge,* 206

Black Blood and *Under the Bridge* are the first two installments in the five book series that makes up Paci's *Kunstlerroman,* his portrait of an artist as a young man. In these two novels and the following three, he traces the development of Mark Trecroci's character and mind, the formation of self and soul, as well as his making as a writer. (Although Mark has not started writing by the end of the second book, it is obviously his true vocation.) The two books cover Trecroci's time in Sault Ste. Marie, those crucial and determining years that stretch from his "first act of conciousness" at five years of age to his graduation from high school at eighteen. *Black Blood* and *Under the Bridge* share not only the same protagonist and setting, but also the same characters, themes, imagery, conflict, and story. They are two parts of one work.

(Whereas, in the next book, *Sex and Character*, many of these elements do change.)

The idea that dominates both books is that of *black blood;* repeatedly, Mark refers to the effect that the printed words on a page have on him: "The new words seemed to have a magical quality that made them jump off the page and stir my blood without making much sense to me . . . My eyes were like sponges soaked in black print" (*Under the Bridge*, 205). He also writes of Shakespeare, Camus and Spinoza: "Their words were their blood which they transported onto a sheet of paper, and which I drank with my thirsty eyes. Their words were their blood, which coursed through my veins, displacing my father's blood . . . "(*Under the Bridge*, 156).

On rereading the two novels, I hazard to say that Paci wants his words to act upon us, the readers, even in some small way, the way the printed words act upon Mark Trecroci. He wants the novels to touch his readers like *a heady elixir*, to enter their bloodstream. And Paci's style reflects that desire. His language is serious, intimate, intense, and moving. His tone is heated rather than cool. We are not distanced from Mark; we are given his experiences with almost no obvious reflection. At the beginning of *Black Blood*, Mark tells us that he is writing from "the middle of my life, equidistant from birth and death" (*Black Blood*, 3). So the narrative we are reading is a looking back by an older, presumably wiser, man on his childhood and youth. Yet, after the opening, the narrator is not self-reflexive; he does not remind us that he is recalling events that happened many years earlier, and that memory can be specious. He does not hold up his other self, the young Mark, and his storms of adolescence as an object of humour. Except for certain elegaic passages about the lost paradise of childhood, Paci presents the young Mark with very little stylistic mediation or irony.

In her book *Splitting Images: Contemporary Canadian Ironies*, Linda Hutcheon states that "irony is one of the discursive strategies used by [such] marginalized or 'minoritarian' artists to signal [that] resistance" (48). Building on Eli Mandel's idea that doubleness and even duplicity is part of an immigrant's daily life and that literature can come from this doubleness, Hutcheon suggests "that irony is one way of coming to terms with this kind of duplicity, for it is the trope that incarnates doubleness," and irony is "an effective tool for articulating both marginalization and the challenge to it" (49).

Hutcheon does not specifically examine the novels of Frank Paci in *Splitting Images*, but she does note that Italian-Canadian writers do not tend to use the power of irony when "dealing with their ethnic roots" (59). She posits two contradictory reasons to explain why the Italian-Canadian writer does not fit the pattern of the ethnic writer. The first suggests that since Italian immigration to Canada is still fairly recent, Italian-Canadian writers need time and distance before they will move out of the mode of loss and mourning. Irony for these writers still seems to be taboo. "Perhaps . . . the experience of Italian immigrants has been more one of suffering, pain, and death than joy – or even resistance" (59). The other contradictory reason is that "Italians in Canada may well now have less cause for the kind of anger that can unleash the true fury of oppositional irony in the responses of other ethnic and racial groups" (59).

I have summarized Linda Hutcheon's position on irony and Italian Canadian writers at length because, like Hutcheon, I found the lack of irony in *Black Blood* and *Under the Bridge* surprising. But when I thought of the effect of Paci's serious style, I realized that Paci's avoidance of stylistic irony was a deliberate aesthetic choice. In *Under the Bridge*, Mark does imagine writing a Dear Rhonda letter to the advice columnist in the Sault paper: "I've contravened all the laws of God," he imagines writing. "My mother can't even speak English" (120). There is humour and irony in his letter and in Rhonda's breezy response, which consists only of cliches. ". . . you need to go out and smell the roses. Stop thinking that you are the centre of the world" (*Under the Bridge*, 120). However, since Paci does not want us to feel distanced from Mark, he uses this device only once. In these first two books on the making of Mark Trecroci, our hero is a typical second-generation ethnic, identifing completely with the Canadian culture. Although Mark feels some hostility to the Americans who flood over the bridge connecting the two countries, the only culture he resists is the Italian peasant culture represented by his parents. (It is his troubled friend Rico, who was older when he arrived from Italy, who feels torn between

Canada and Italy. Significantly, Rico is an outsider, a convict, and a dropout, who finds peace only when he is living alone in the wilderness.)

Still, although we are caught up in the young Mark's point of view, we are told at the beginning that this book is a confession; he is telling the story of his "sins and moments of being, easily retraceable as the pivotal points in anyone's life" (*Black Blood*, 3). And though we see his parents and sister through Mark's eyes, we see that his anger and his cold treatment of them are indeed sins.

He also says that he is not modeling his work on modern confessions, but on the "Great Explorers of the past" (*Black Blood*, 3), and in his narrative he alludes to explorers of both inner and outer worlds. The form of Mark's confession and its emphasis are inspired by the philosophers of late antiquity, specifically Plotinus, a Neo-Platonist, and St. Augustine. "It's not a journey for feet, says Plotinus" (*Black Blood* 3), but for the mind and the soul. Plotinus used his personal experience to delineate a philosophy whereby knowledge of the One and the Good can be obtained first through intuitive thought and then by an ecstatic contemplation. Mark aspires to the Good and to be good. Like Plotinus, about whom his biographer said "He seemed ashamed of being in a body" (*The Oxford Companion to Classical Literature*, 447), Mark longs to be freed of his material self, hating his acne and sexual impulses.

One of the most important events in *Black Blood*, one that reverberates through both books, is Mark

and his friends' robbery of fruit from the Stone
Garden, and it strongly evokes a central incident in
The Confessions of St. Augustine, wherein Augustine
and his friends steal fruit. Of course, forbidden fruit
and a lush, enclosed garden also evoke the garden of
Eden and the fall. Significantly, on first seeing this
"shangri-la," Rico blurts out, "just like Italia" (*Black
Blood*, 69). Mark's first "moment of being," his first
sexual experience, occurs close to the walls of the
Stone Garden and is always associated in his mind
with the garden. When Mark and his friends climb
over the wall, they steal apples; Augustine and his
friends steal pears. But what Augustine says about
himself and his feeling of elation after stealing the
pears is true also for Mark and his feeling of elation
after taking the apples: "All my enjoyment was in the
theft itself and in the sin" (*The Confessions of St.
Augustine*, 45). And both can say I "loved the com-
pany of those with whom I committed [the sin]"
(*Confessions*, 50).

Again, it is striking how un-ironic and unusual
Paci is in his use of earlier texts. These novels were
written in the early nineties when the deconstruction
of the classics was fashionable, but Paci's intertextu-
ality is not post-modern. There are no implied quo-
tation marks setting off the confessions of Mark
Trecroci.

Likewise, Mark sees himself (with no irony) as
following the great explorers of the outer world:
Columbus, Cabot, Radisson, and Brule. And Paci
gives Mark the last name Trecroci, three crosses,

which evokes the three crosses on Mount Calvary. In his earlier years, Mark Trecroci is often in church contemplating the crucifix, the image of Christ on the cross. He fails at being good, being Christ-like. Yet he casts himself as a hero none the less. "From the itchiness of my face it felt as if the Crucified Christ from Mount Carmel was pecking away like a vulture" (*Under the Bridge*, 51). Here he manages to see himself as a Promethean figure, punished by God rather than Zeus.

The coming of age and art of a white male, who models himself on and judges himself by the early classics of Western civilization, is hardly a fashionable subject for a novel these days. And this absence of fashionable subject and fashionable irony is partly responsible, I feel, for these two novels not receiving the attention and appreciation they deserve. In *A Reader's Manifesto*, a recent attack on "the growing pretentiousness of American literary prose," B.R. Myers argues: "Even the most obvious triteness is acceptable, provided it comes with a postmodern wink" (*The Atlantic Monthly*, 104). He also claims that the most highly acclaimed styles of contemporary writing are often obscure, repetitive, or "a jumble of unsustained metaphors" (*Atlantic*, 105). The literary climate is similar in Canada. Writers of what I call gauzy or hazy fiction, prose that is very difficult for the reader to perceive what is going on, these writers are the ones that are most praised for their so-called lyrical style. Myers argues: "Everything is *in*, as long as it keeps the reader at a respectfully admiring *dis-*

tance" (emphasis mine, *Atlantic*, 104). As noted above, Paci's style is aimed at canceling the distance between reader and text. Even without considering the presence or lack of irony, Paci's prose style is unfashionable.

His style is transparent and realistic; it does not draw attention to itself. It reflects the weight of Mark's world, the presence of the things within it, including the Italian West-end, St. Mary's canal, the steel plant, the chrome plant, the paper mill, the CPR tracks, the railroad bridge, the ballpark, the hockey rink, Mount Carmel church, the Circle of boulders, the Stone Garden, the grasslands, and the caves. Italo Calvino wrote of six values or qualities of literature that must be retained in the new millenium. Paci's style demonstrates the value that Calvino calls exactitude, which he relates to the practice of poets and their precision. When Mark Trecroci describes his father's hands, he does so with exactitude, noting what those hands can do and recording each scar, and how they were made "by a hammer . . . by a rotary blade" (*Under the Bridge*, 13). "Large stubby hands they were for his size, with bulging veins at the back, short fingers that flattened out into wide nails cracked by years of labour" (*Under the Bridge*, 12). Through the exactitude of his description, Paci communicates Mark's repressed love for his father. Mark may be embarrassed by his father; he may sneer at him, but through the exactitude, we sense the strength and dignity of the father. We are moved by him.

In denying us the distancing effect of irony which

would allow us to smile at Mark, and perhaps to place him, Paci instead uses language that is serious, exact, and intimate, thus allowing us to both identify with Mark and to judge him harshly. Reading the two books, I found myself both sympathizing with Mark and being furious with him. I wanted to scream at him and make him see how much pain he was inflicting on his sister, mother, and father.

I must conclude that Paci's stylistic choices in *Black Blood* and *Under the Bridge* were deliberate. He wanted to involve us, to move us, and then he wanted us to make judgements, to understand the struggle and the hurt between immigrant father and Canadian son.

I think he succeeds.

WORKS CITED

Augustine, Saint, *Bishop of Hippo The Confessions of St. Augustine*, tr. Rex Warner New York: New American Library, 1963.

Calvino, Italo *Six Memos for the Next Millenium* Cambridge, Massachusetts: Harvard University Press, 1988.

Howatson, M.C. ed. *The Oxford Companion to Classical Literature*. Second Edition. Oxford: Oxford University Press, 1989. p. 447

Hutcheon, Linda. *Splitting Images: Contemporary Canadian Ironies*. Toronto: Oxford U.P. 1991.

Myers, B. R. "A Reader's Manifesto," *The Atlantic Monthly*, 288, No 1, July-Aug. 2001, p. 104-122.

Paci, F. G. *Black Blood*, Ottawa: Oberon Press, 1991.

——. *Under the Bridge*, Ottawa: Oberon Press, 1992.

SEARCH FOR THE GREAT MOTHER

ROBERTA SCIFF-ZAMARO

The relationship between Assunta and Marie had always been problematic. It is especially through the extensive flash-backs leading us through Marie's childhood and adolescence that we acquire an understanding of the difficulties between the two women.

*

If Marie's psychology is clearly portrayed in the novel, Assunta instead appears as its most enigmatic character who, however, must not be dismissed before a closer analysis.

Adamo's death appears to be decisive for the following development of the story since it affects Assunta so strongly as to take away from her any desire to keep on living. The title itself, *Black Madonna*, refers to this figure of a woman who, at her husband's death, decides to wear the deepest mourning, thus following one of the fundamental dictates of the culture she belongs to . . .

*

It is in Marie's quest to find her true self out of a split identity that the archetype of the Great Mother emerges investing the quest with a mythological di-

mension. When mentioning the archetype of the
Great Mother we are referring to the primordial
feminine principle present in the collective unconscious. As Erich Neumann observes in his *The Great
Mother*, the female principle appears to have a double
nature; on the one hand it is inherent in the psyche
itself, on the other hand it manifests itself through the
projections of images or symbols:

> When analytical psychology speaks of the primordial im-
> age or archetype of the Great Mother, it is referring, not
> to any concrete image existing in space and time, but to
> an inward image at work in the human psyche. The sym-
> bolic expression of this psychic phenomenon is to be
> found in the figures of the Great Goddess represented in
> the myths and artistic creations of mankind. The effect of
> this archetype may be followed through the whole of his-
> tory for we can demonstrate its workings in the rites,
> myths, symbols, of early man and also in the dreams, fan-
> tasies, and creative works of the sound as well as the sick
> man of our own day. (3)

The fact that *Black Madonna* represents a projection
of the archetype of the Great Mother is already hinted
by the title itself. On a literal level, Assunta becomes
the "black madonna" because of the morning after
her husband's death; such a connotation, however,
has a far-reaching effect when we deal on a symbolic
level. Again Erich Neumann points out:

> The term Great Mother, as a partial aspect of the Arche-
> typal Feminine, is a late abstraction, presupposing a
> highly developed speculative consciousness. And indeed,
> it is only relatively late in the history of mankind that we

find the Archetypal Feminine designated as Magna Mater. But it was worshiped and portrayed many thousands of years before the appearance of the term. (11)

Thus the figure of the Great Mother, or Great Goddess, happens to have been extensively worshiped much earlier than the coinage of the term itself. As Robert Graves observes in *The White Goddess*, at first the Great Goddess was the only power to be worshiped but later on, with the advent of the institution of monogamy, her role became less influential and she was reduced to consort of the Father-God (389). The most striking change took place, however, in the Judaic and Christian societies as well as, generally speaking, in every society based on patriarchy. In the Christian mythology we can observe a radical subversion of the Great Goddess myth. It would be proper, in fact, to point out at this stage that the figure of the Great Mother has a three-fold nature; in her first manifestation she presents herself as the white goddess of birth and growth; in her second, as the red goddess of battle and love; in her third one, as the black goddess of death and divination. In Christian mythology the triple Goddess is almost completely effaced as such, and it is substituted by a God, triple in nature himself. Her figure, however, is still present in Christian mythology in the person of Mary, purged of course of any connotation referring to her original status, who is relegated to the role of Mother of God. However, her very name is a reminiscence of an ancient sea-goddess who was nothing else but the

Great Goddess herself under a different form. As Graves points out, "the charming Virgin with the blue robe and pearl necklace was the ancient pagan Sea-goddess Marian in transparent disguise – Marian, Miriam, Marianne (*Sea Lamb*) Myrrhine, Myrtea, Myrrha, Maria or Marina, patroness of poets and lovers and proud mother of the Archer of Love" (394-95). When we identify in Mary, mother of God, the figure of the Great Mother, the connection between the latter and the "black madonna" is clear if we note that in Italian "La Madonna" is another name used to define the Mother of God. Moreover, it would not be out of place to notice here that the statue of the Virgin in procession, referred to in the novel in relation to Marie's past, recalls Grave's sea-goddess in disguise: "The bier holding the large statue of Our Lady of Mount Carmel . . . Our Lady in powder-blue and white holding a scapular medal in her outstretched hand, and dollar bills pasted like wreaths around her neck" (25).

Returning to the figure of the "black madonna," her attribute of "black" is another hint at the Great Mother and, more precisely, her black phase, the Hecate phase, connected with death and the underworld and again referred to by Graves as the Black Goddess, or Goddess of Wisdom, mysterious sister of the White Goddess. In this context the critic makes an interesting reference to the Sicilian "black virgins," a term which could easily be replaced by "black madonnas," since in the Christian tradition madonna implies virgin, and so called "because they derive

from an ancient tradition of Wisdom as Blackness"
(*Mammon*, 162). In our novel the black madonna is
represented by Assunta, the mysterious, almost sibylline character who appears to her daughter as a
monster. In her quest for an identity, Marie constantly finds an obstacle in the overpowering figure
of her mother. During her childhood, the monster
appears as an actual tyrant who has imprisoned Marie
on two levels, a physical one represented by her
fatness, and a psychological one, represented by her
Italian environment she feels is alien. During her
maturity, Assunta turns into a ghost haunting her
mind.

The image of the mother turned into a phantom
of her daughter's mind reappears in different Canadian novels by women writers. In each case this image
always represents the projection of the black goddess
entrapped inside and who needs to be released to
reach an identity. If we consider for a moment Margaret Atwood's *Lady Oracle*, we see that Joan, the
heroine, is portrayed as searching for her real self, and
throughout the quest is constantly haunted by the
figure of her mother who is again represented as a
tyrant during Joan's childhood, and as a phantom of
her psyche in her adulthood. Although Joan has
succeeded in freeing herself from her mother's influence in a physical sense, namely by getting rid of her
fatness and by moving to a complete new life, her
mother, nevertheless, has become an obsession on a
psychological level. She has turned into a projection
of Joan's fears to become a reflection of her own

mother. In a first moment Joan does not realize that she cannot reject the figure of her mother since the latter is part of her own self, which again refers to the archetype Great Mother. Once the Goddess lost most of her power and was reduced to the Father-God's consort, the daughters she had from him were "limited versions of herself – herself in various young-moon and full-moon aspects" (Graves, 389) . . .

Moving to another Canadian novel, Anne Hébert's *Kamouraska*, we notice that its heroine, Elisabeth, is involved in a search for identity which again refers to the same archetype. The search always takes place in a state of drowsiness, and in all her visions Elisabeth always sees her mother standing beside her. Even though such a figure is not so obsessive as that of Joan's mother, it nevertheless presents many characterisitics of the black goddess. She is described as always wearing black robes, *costumée en gran-mère* (52) even when she is only seventeen and, moreover, as trying to foretell the future. Elisabeth herself is portrayed as a projection of the black goddess she has inside and who she must release in order to discover her true identity and start a new life.

The same pattern followed by Joan to free herself in *Lady Oracle* reappears in *Black Madonna*. Although in due time Marie is able to free herself in a literal sense by getting away from her family, and especially from her mother's influence, to begin a new life by herself, the attained freedom turns out to be an incomplete one. As soon as she moves to Toronto,

Marie begins to undergo a process of metamorphosis which is intended to efface anything which links her to her past and in particular to her mother. The first step toward her new identity is to get rid of her fatness, imposed on her by Assunta, which implies the rejection of food. "Since her first year at university she had stopped eating Italian food altogether. Later it wasn't only Italian food, but anything having to do with her mother's dishes" (100). The rejection of food symbolizes the rejection of the mother herself, who has always been associated first of all with eating.

From this process of metamorphosis Marie comes out completely changed; she is a new person with not links with her Italian origins: "She had shed her odious cocoon, looked bone-thin and gloriously herself " (97). The break is not only represented in her physical appearance but also in the fact that she chooses a different kind of life; she decides to be a "woman professor," and not the traditional wife and mother she was supposed to become according to Assunta's canons. Although she is able to free herself in a physical sense, her mother continues to pursue her and turns into an obsession. At the very moment Marie is completely sure to have disentangled herself from Assunta, the latter begins to appear to her under the form of hallucinations. The first instance of Assunta's return is offered by the scene in which Marie is victim of a presumed swoon during which everything she has been trying to reject for so long, imposes on her with utmost strength. In her vision Marie sees her mother's Christmas table regally set out; she is attracted towards it as if towards a magnet, and from it she derives an inexplicable pleasure. Since the scene mentioned has a highly sexual import, its meaning is far-reaching. On a rational level Marie has refused everything connected with her origins, but in her unconscious the food, which does not represent anything but a symbol of her mother and, therefore, of her own nature as well, turns out to be a fundamental part of her own self; it is something she really needs and desires, and from which she feels highly rewarded. All the marks of her origins that she has tried to efface for so long have overcome her in a moment when her subconscious, her true inner self, gains an advantage over her, she is lead to give vent to her sensuality, her womanhood, which she has tried to suffocate since her adolescence as something too primitive, too Italian.

Later on Marie actually feels her mother's return: "At that moment Marie felt the unmistakable presence of her mother's dark figure in the room . . . Marie got up and looked at herself in the mirror. Her face was old and ravaged. It was as if her mother were staring back at her" (116-17). Marie just begins to realize that she cannot reject the figure of her mother since the latter is part of herself. What is fighting in her is the Hecate figure, the black goddess, but she is unable to accept it since she still does not have a full perception of it.

This is an excerpt from the longer essay, "*Black Madonna: A Search for the Great Mother*," which originally appeared in *Contrasts* (1985).

WORKS CITED

Atwood, Margaret. *Lady Oracle*. Toronto: McLelland & Stewart, 1976.

Hébert, Anne. *Kamouraska*. Paris: Seuil, 1970.

Graves, Robert. *The White Goddess*. New York: Farrar, Straus & Giroux, 1966.

_____. *Mammon and the Black Goddess*. New York: Doubleday, 1965.

Neumann, Erich. *The Great Mother: An Analysis of an Archetype*. New York: Bollingen, 1955.

Paci, F.G. *Black Madonna*. Ottawa: Oberon, 1982.

Ed. Note: See Lucia Chiavola Birnbaum, *Black Madonnas: Feminism, Religion and Politics in Italy*. Ithaca: Northeastern University Press, 1993.

"THE OLD COUNTRY IN YOUR BLOOD"

Italy and Canada in Frank Paci's Black Madonna *and Margaret Atwood's* Lady Oracle

ENOCH PADOLSKY

In his 1985 interview with C.D. Minni (*Canadian Literature* 106: 5-15), Frank Paci notes that his own "return journey" to Italy in 1972 acted as a crucial "catalyst that finally made me see that I had to come to terms with my Italian background before I could write about anything else" (6). "Canadians of Italian descent," he goes on, "should look overseas to get a more complete sense of their identities" (7). Paci's insight here, it seems to me, is not about Italy as such, but rather about how to acquire both intellectual and emotional *perspective* on the questions of identity and ontology that are faced by Italian-Canadian immigrants, and especially by their second generation Canadian children. What Paci is most concerned with is the generational problems that arise in the new land ("la via vecchia" versus "la via nuova" (Minni, 9), and in the difficulties of inter-generational understanding and communication. At the same time, though Paci writes fully out of this Italian-Canadian experience, it is fair to say that he also sees himself as an artist who is addressing more general Canadian and universal issues. As he puts it in another 1985 essay, "Tasks of the Canadian Novelist Writing on Immigrant Themes," his fictional characters and the families they form, only "happened to be of Italian descent. The family was the major focus." (49). The psychological dynamics that Paci aims to explore, from *The Italians* (1978) onwards, thus can be said to derive from Italian-Canadian experience but also to have much broader implications for individuals, for families and for communities in general. His themes include a wide range of artistic and human problematics – the centrality of family and community, the role of the artist and the relationship of art to form, the connection between mind and body, "the transmission of deeply felt experience" ("Tasks," 47). To treat these themes successfully and honestly, Paci states, the writer has to "dig deep in his own self" (*loc cit.*), including, as the first citation and my title suggest, understanding where your family and culture come from. In Paci's case, this has led to a remarkable series of novels which has brought to life the rich duality of Italian-Canadian experience, and in which his characters confront in their lives the significance of both Italy and Canada, and the troublesome interplay between them.

In the discussion that follows, I would like to explore Paci's analysis of the nature of the Italian-Canadian duality in the light of these more universal issues. In particular, I am interested in how Paci's ethnic minority positioning is reflected in how he approaches and frames these questions. But just as Paci looks to Italy as a way of providing perspective on the Canadian experience of his second generation characters, I would like to look to the writing of a very "mainstream" ethnic majority writer as a way of providing perspective on Paci. The writer I have in mind is Margaret Atwood and the work that is most pertinent to Paci is her 1976 novel *Lady Oracle*, a work which Paci may very well have known. In any case, Atwood's novel contains some remarkable parallels to Paci's thematics and because it provides a British-Canadian *majority* perspective on these issues, it also provides a way of seeing how Paci's treatment of Italy and Canada is itself derived from his own particular minority perspective. For Paci, I would like to focus on his second novel, *Black Madonna* (1982), and in particular, his treatment of the mother-daughter relationship in it. Of all Paci's novels, it is perhaps *Black Madonna* which most poignantly captures the emotional turmoil of these issues of identity and ontology. I have taught this novel for many years and have found that students never fail to react to it in a visceral way. Solidly based in the realities of post-war Sault Ste. Marie, with its dominating Steel Mill and declining West End neighbourhood, *Black Madonna* portrays an immigrant Italian-Canadian family caught up in a crisis of intergenerational perspectives, of conflict between parents and children over what it means to be in Canada and also to be of Italian descent. The antagonistic relationship between the daughter Marie and the mother

Assunta is especially poignant and it is this relationship that offers the most interesting basis of comparison with Atwood's novel, for *Lady Oracle* also features a female character (Joan Foster) in search of her identity who is caught in an ongoing battle with her mother. In addition, Atwood's novel happens to be set in Italy (the present time of the plot), and when it looks back to the past in Canada and England, it also makes some interesting cross-cultural comparisons between mainstream and minority cultures. Let me begin, then, with a look at how Atwood's novel handles Canada and Italy, starting with the tempestuous relationship between mother and daughter in that work.

As in Paci's novel, the terms of the battle between Joan and her mother in *Lady Oracle* are cultural. Joan's mother attempts to impose on her the culturally stereotypical feminine role of "American" culture (Joan Crawford, etc.) in its Canadian (i.e. British-Canadian) middle-class, upwardly mobile version of tidiness, emotional control, Brownies, etc. (Cf. the analysis of Gayle Wurst.) Interestingly, the mother-daughter struggle takes place on the same battleground as in *Black Madonna* – the daughter's body: "The war between myself and my mother was on in earnest; the disputed territory was my body" (67). Yet if the two novels accord on the terrain of the generational battle, they differ significantly in the tactics of rebellion of the daughters. While Marie refuses to eat her mother's Italian food in order to become thin and "English," the young Joan in *Lady Oracle* eats incessantly in order to become "fat" (Atwood's term), thereby thwarting the controlling hand of the mother and the dominant mainstream cultural image of women. Atwood then goes on, in numerous ways, to explore the consequences, social and psychological, of this cultural non-conformity, and uses the presence of the "fat woman" in the novel as a site of commentary on Canadian patriarchal culture. Among other things, what Joan finds is that her "fatness" makes her sexually invisible to her British-Canadian peers, both male and female.

That Atwood's Canadian cultural parameters are "ethnic majority" in nature is established because Atwood overtly contextualizes them within the novel in relation to both ethnic minority (immigrant) characters and "foreign" places. Thus Joan's struggle for control of her body, as well as her quest for identity and for place in Canadian culture (her relations with men, with art, with politics) are not limited to mainstream Canadian cultural space. In Toronto, Joan encounters immigrant characters who see her quite differently, and her story takes her not only to England (and a Polish "count"), but to Italy where the present time of the novel, which both opens and closes the story, is set. These crossings of cultural boundaries are not the central action of the novel but they do serve to provide a variety of cultural alternatives and thereby a defining of the limits of the dominant culture. The main focus in the novel, however, the interior world of experience from which the novel is written, remains clearly Canadian ethnic majority, and the main characters all fall into this cultural space. Her father grew up in Rosedale, "that stomping ground of respectable Anglo-Saxon money" (179), her upwardly mobile mother wants her to go to Trinity College (93), and Joan frequently uses the Queen as a reference point in her life (cf. 9). Indeed, to judge by the names of her lovers and literary creations, Joan's interest in Royalty is pervasive: the Polish Count, (King) Arthur, the Royal Porcupine, and all the lords and ladies of her Costume Gothic books, even including, I assume, "Lady Oracle" herself (with the Lady of Shalott in the background). As her lover, the Royal Porcupine, explains: "I'm a Royalist . . . I really dig the Queen. . . . It's like the Royal Mail or the Royal Canadian Mounted Police" (241-2). This attachment to English roots makes Joan's journey to England into a kind of "return journey" to the ethnic homeland, but her culture is Canadian, not British. She may romantically prefer the exoticism of the Polish count or at least of a "British accent," but her one true love turns out to be "unfortunately . . . only a Canadian, like [her]" (165). Canadian, of course, means British-Canadian.

Set against this British-Canadian majority cultural space in the novel, non-British-Canadian immigrant culture in Toronto and Italian "foreign" space provide a contrasting context of otherness. Thus, returning to Joan's "fatness," and its concomitant sexual invisibility, one of Joan's first insights about the cultural limits of her own identity is to discover that these assumptions about female appearance are not universal, even in Toronto. The fleshy Joan discovers this when she is pursued by an immigrant, who refuses to recognize the non-sexual status British-Canadian culture ascribes to "fat ladies" and who even proposes marriage to her. For Joan, this experience becomes both part of her sexual awakening and also of the formation of her ethnic (majority) identity. Note that Atwood's interest in this immigrant man, (like Paci's interest in Marie's husband, as we shall see), is secondary and primarily external. Joan's immigrant suitor is described in contrast to "a lethargic, resentful Canadian" as "a sprightly, bright-eyed foreigner, either Italian or Greek, I wasn't sure which" (98). Even his old-country name, a tell-tale sign of cultural significance, is omitted, and we are told that "in his determination to become a Canadian, he insisted that it was John" (100). Later in the novel he appears as "Zerdo," cashing in on Canadian multiculturalism with his exotic "ethnic" restaurant. Zerdo's ethnic identity (and all the issues that go with it) are thus not important to Joan or to Atwood, except by way of contrast. From the majority perspective of the novel, Canadian society seems to be peopled by two categories – Canadians and "foreigners." For Joan (and for Atwood), the content of immigrant experience is irrelevant, is all the same, is unreal, is "ethnic," is merely a contrast to the presumed complex and real experience of the largely unconscious and dominant British-Canadian majority ethnicity.

Towards the end of the novel, there is a scene which reveals this perspective very clearly, and which

illustrates as well, the power and subtlety of majority
dominance in Canadian society. Joan, now a thin and
successful writer in "mainstream" Canadian society,
sits at the table in Zerdo's restaurant with the same
(foreign) "Polish" count she met earlier in London, is
waited upon obsequiously by John-Zerdo her former
"bright-eyed" foreign (Italian or Greek) suitor, looks
at his current "fat" unnamed "ethnic" wife (whom she
might have been), and comparing the assumed simplicity of the latter's life with the disturbing complexity of her own, thinks to herself: "At this moment, I
envied her" (281). Now Margaret Atwood, as we all
know, is a satirist and she may be satirizing Joan from
a pluralistic perspective in this scene. Nevertheless,
satire or not, this novelistic moment of "ethnic"
generosity and "envy" illustrates very clearly one
form of an ethnic majority perspective in relation to
minority cultures in Canada. In a Paci novel such as
Black Madonna, as we shall see, it is precisely the
perspective of that immigrant woman that is at the
centre, and as the discussion of Paci's novel that
follows makes amply evident, the life of that immigrant woman is hardly "simple" and certainly not to
be envied. Such is the difference between an ethnic
minority and an ethnic majority perspective on that
experience.

The Italian setting of *Lady Oracle* follows a similar
pattern. For Atwood's character Joan, Italy is an
escape, and is chosen by her not just because she had
visited it previously with her husband Arthur but
because it is far away from Canada and far removed

from British-Canadian culture. Atwood could presumably have had Joan escape to London, where she
lived for much longer before and after she had met
Arthur. But England is perceived as not far enough
away, i.e. too culturally accessible to Canada. Italy is
not. The choice of Italy is thus again culturally significant because of its difference. Joan's aim is to hide, to
lose herself in otherness, and, as her fantasies reveal,
this otherness not only provides camouflage, it also
offers the exotic and erotic appeal of her former
"non-Canadian" liaisons:

> I could merge into Italy, marry a vegetable man: we'd live
> in a little stone cottage, I'd have babies and fatten up, we'd
> eat steamy food and cover our bodies with oil, we'd laugh
> at death and live in the present, I'd wear my hair in a bun
> and grow a moustache . . . (334)

This is, needless to say, totally an outsider's comic
perspective on Italian culture and all it reveals is
Joan's inability to enter into or to understand Italian
reality, except in the most stereotypical way. As she
puts it herself, it is no more than a fantasy of being a
"predatory female tourist" (312). In a similar fashion,
Joan's contorted relations with her kind landlord and
her evaluation of the women in the village (the black
Madonnas of Paci's novel!) as culturally threatening,
also reflect her touristic understanding of Italy. The
point, of course, is not that Atwood herself sees Italy
stereotypically (she is clearly satirizing Joan on this
point), but that she (and her main character) only
have an interest in Italy and Italian culture insofar as

they provide a context for the Canadian ethnic majority culture which is the central focus of the novel's experience. Unlike Italian-Canadian writers like Paci (or Edwards, Minni, Micone, etc.), Italy in Atwood's novel is not meaningful in itself and in its Italy-Canada history. It is mere backdrop, otherness, difference. It could presumably, just as easily (to quote Joan on John/Zerdo again) have been Greece. The significance of Italy in the novel is thus not that it is Italy, but that it is able to reveal something about British-Canadian culture which Joan, Atwood and Atwood's assumed British-Canadian reader would not otherwise notice or learn.

In Atwood's *Lady Oracle*, then, Italy and Canada are both reflected through the lens of a British-Canadian mental and emotional space. The immigrants in Canada (or England) provide perspective for Atwood's character Joan on her own cultural roots, and the escape to Italy in the end does no more than delay her encounter with her own ghosts: "I was here in a beautiful southern landscape, with breezes and old world charm, but all the time my old country [Canada] was embedded in my brain . . ." (311). Or to put it in terms of language, the Italian typewriter Joan buys does not work for her because it has a different keyboard and available alphabet (194). To resolve her psychological and personal problems, Joan needs to travel, not to Italy per se, but inwards and ultimately she needs to return to Canada and her own social and cultural space. Atwood's aim in *Lady Oracle*, as in many of her works, is precisely to highlight this need of going inwards, going "underground" into one's own psyche and culture in order to establish one's own stability and identity. Joan, like Marie in *Black Madonna*, must come to terms with her mother and her own culture. Italy and immigrant cultural assumptions can only provide a means of seeing this.

Atwood's treatment of Italy and Canada in *Lady Oracle* provides a useful comparative context for our consideration of Paci's *Black Madonna*. Just as Joan Foster gives Atwood the opportunity to explore the cultural problematics of mainstream female British-Canadian experience, the character of Marie Barone in *Black Madonna* illustrates the Italian-Canadian cultural dilemmas that interest Paci and the interior (ethnic minority) perspective that he brings to bear on them in the novel. As a young girl growing up in Canadian space, Marie sees herself caught in an intolerable situation, part of a family and a culture which she can no longer identify with, and tied to a mother with whom she constantly battles. Her alienation leads to a severely dysfunctional family situation. Her "blinding hatred of her mother" (74), her sense of shame and self-hatred, lead her to flee the "sickening Italian voices" (66) of her home, and to think of herself "as a foreigner in her own house" (66). As part of her rejection of family and Italian background, Marie refuses her mother's insistent attempts to overwhelm her with food (to overcome the influence of "the English and their stupid eating habits" 32), she changes her name from Maria to the more "Canadian" Marie, abandons all things Italian, including the

Church, and leaves the cultural restrictions (in her view) of the West End Sault for the more liberating locale of urban Toronto. There, against her parents' older generation Italian working class assumptions about education for women, she goes to university, and ends up marrying an English-Canadian Protestant in an "Anglican chapel" (140). Her "assimilation" is so complete that at one point when she is teaching school, an Italian-Canadian student in her class, unaware of her origins, accuses her of prejudice against Italians.

The situation that Marie represents, for Paci, is a kind of second generational internal colonization, in the sense that her entire psychology has aligned itself with the world of the "English-speaking country" and all that that entails, against the "Italian-speaking house" (69) of family, community, language and cultural heritage. What the novel explores, and not just for Marie, is the reason for, the dynamics of, and the cost of this psychological state for all concerned. Paci's treatment of these issues is rich with nuance, with irony, with judgment and with affection. Marie's rejection of her mother's food, for example, can be seen as part of her rebellion against her mother, against Italy, and against the pre-set traditional female role of "devoted Italian wife" (25). At the same time, it is anorexic, fanatically incorrect (spaghetti is also part of British-Canadian cuisine) and it correlates with dominant (patriarchal) British-Canadian cultural valuing of thinness. To bring back our previous comparison with *Lady Oracle*, in matters of food,

Marie is siding with Joan's mother not with Joan. But the cultural battleground is reversed. To resist *her* mother, Marie chooses to lose weight, not put it on. That Paci is playing with the ironies of this cultural situation is evident at the end of the novel, when the "rebelliously" thin Marie fits perfectly into her mother's (Italian) black dress. Significantly, Marie's long unhealthy rejection of food finally becomes the means to understanding, reconciliation, and new insight into her own Italian identity (and family) past.

Paci's treatment of Marie, as in the case of her brother Joey, fleshes out (literally and metaphorically) the implications of the cultural tensions within Italian-Canadian experience as he sees it. Marie's escape into the perceived "English" world of abstract reason, mathematics and logic at the expense of her "Italian" blood, body and emotions, become for Paci a trope for the divisions within Italian-Canadian experience on individual, family and community levels. The division of mind from body that Marie strives for has dire consequences at all levels of her life. Such an unhealthy split is actually hard to maintain, as the incident with the Lebanese student (110 ff.), what Paci elsewhere calls "the lurking presence of the crotch" ("Tasks," 58), illustrates. For Marie, a divided mind and body affects her health, her marriage, her relationship with both her parents and her son, and even her career. Thus Marie's attempt to teach mathematics and logic to her high school students as an "analytical method," a "totally impersonal tool" that "made them rise above such divisive things as language and background and emotion" leads not to their achieving "mastery over their own fate" (139), as she expects, but rather to the misunderstanding that she dislikes Italians. This divisiveness, one can infer, is unhealthy and unwise for the individuals concerned, and unfortunate, even tragic, for generational understanding and community relations. In the novel, the untimely death of the father, the violent dismemberment of the Black Madonna mother, and by extension, the decay and destruction of the West End in general, all illustrate the impact (symbolic and real) of the cultural breakdown of the continuity between body and mind, parents and children, old world and new world, Italy and Canada, that constitutes the cost of immigration to the older generation and their community.

Yet if the distance between forehead and chest is the "longest yard in existence", as Father Kiley tells Stephen in Paci's next novel (*The Father*, 94), it is a distance that ultimately must be bridged if health and reconciliation are ever to be re-established. At the end of *Black Madonna*, Marie's promise of a "return journey" to Italy, the re-established continuity of the Hope Chest which she takes back to Italy, the symbolic (if belated) reconciliation to her parents through Joey at the end of the novel, and her apology to her mother (192) all hold out hope of such a bridging of heart and mind at all these levels. On Joey's side, a similar reconciliation takes place, through Marie, through his girlfriend Annalise, and through his father's carpentry and bricklaying tools. The constructed pyramid of bricks which ends the novel asserts the dignity and value of the immigrant genera- tion in the face of inevitable decline but also forms a symbolic linking of the generations. Marie and Joey may never fully understand their "Black Madonna" mother (or Italian father) but ultimately each seems to find a way to move on with their lives in the Canadian context while affirming some aspects of their parental and Italian past.

This brief overview of Marie and the issues of *Black Madonna* does not do justice to the complexity of the novel. Much more could be said, for example, about Paci's depiction of the mother Assunta, or about Joey's struggle with dilemmas that are similar to those of Marie. Yet even from this brief discussion, it is possible to see how Paci's view of *italianità* in the Canadian context flows directly from his deep under- standing of the conflicts within ethnic minority expe- rience. In *Black Madonna*, unlike the case of *Lady Oracle*, "Italy" carries rich cultural, social, and psy- chological significance. In many ways, it is at the heart of the novel's conflicts and insights. The "open" mystery of the Black Madonna, symbolized by the open hope chest, can be "solved" by entering the past, confronting the realities and values of Italian culture, by coming to terms with "the old country in your blood," as Father Sarlo puts it (186). Assunta's back- ground of rural poverty in Italy helps explain her fixation on feeding her children, and her upbringing in rural southern Italy also helps to explain her inabil- ity to adjust to the "modern" Canadian social world in the way that her children wish her to. In an ironic mirroring of Assunta's attempts to understand Canada in her television "pictures", Joey and Marie finally succeed in "seeing" themselves in Assunta's photos of rural Italy, and they come to recognize their mother's voice in the dialect accent of their relatives in the telephone call to Italy. When Marie, dressed in Assunta's black dress, leaves on the plane, Joey notes that she "looked very Italian" and also that she "didn't look out of place" (198). That Assunta dies before her children come to terms with this past only points out the tragedy of her life, and at the same time, the centrality that Paci gives to her situation. In spite of the fact that the novel is written from the children's second generation perspective, it is Assunta, (and *italianità*), as the title suggests, that dominates the problematics of the novel's world.

It should be noted that Paci's ethnic minority perspective is also revealed in the way he handles the dominant (British-Canadian) culture in the novel. This culture is represented in part by Marie's English-Canadian husband Richard, who, significantly, is presented only sketchily and externally. Like the psychiatrist "of British descent" (153) that Joey takes his mother to, Richard stands outside of the interior Italian-Canadian world of the main characters in the novel. He is sympathetic but limited in his understanding of Marie's state. His main function thus seems to be to act as a contrast to the Italian-Canadian culture depicted in the novel, as an outside commentator on Marie's physical and psychological state, and in Paci's depiction of their marriage, of the gender dilemmas (patriarchy) in mainstream Canadian society (as opposed to the traditional patriarchy in the Italian-Canadian family). In the end, he tells Marie that "Italy is something you have to come to terms with on your own" (187) but significantly, he says this "in his pedantic tone." The case of Richard, then, might seem to suggest that Paci's interest in British-Canadian culture is a kind of mirror image of Atwood's use of immigrants and Italy in *Lady Oracle*, namely that he is more interested in its impact on Italian-Canadian experience than in itself. Yet while it is true that the dominant culture provides an outside context for Paci's characters (as the immigrant culture does in Atwood's novel), in another sense, Paci's depiction of the other side of the cultural duality is fundamentally different from that of Atwood. In ethnic minority experience, as Marie's situation illustrates, the dominant culture is *internalized*, becomes more and more important in the lives of the second and subsequent Canadian generations. Indeed, this is what lies at the heart of the problem between the generations. In Atwood's novel there is no such process for Joan and this is what marks the difference between dominant and minority situations.

For Paci, and for his second generation characters, Canada, not Italy, is the primary home. What Paci investigates (obviously not just through Richard, but through hockey, art, history and other elements) is the attractiveness of British-Canadian culture and Canadian place to the younger generations of Italian-

Canadians, the material advantages that lie in moving into dominant society, and the role that they as Canadians will come to play in the new country. For they clearly are Canadians, though they are also "of Italian descent." If Joey's hockey friend and mentor Donny Belsito can make it to the pros, then any of them can. "He charted the map for us." (129), Joey says. In contrast to Assunta, even some first generation Italian-Canadians realize this new unavoidable reality and are able to adjust to it. Thus the widow Angeline, unlike Assunta, notes that she can never leave Canada to go back to Italy: "It's been too long for me. Here is where my children and grandchildren are" (120). Canada and British-Canadian dominant culture are thus not just mirrors in Paci or other minority writers for that matter. Italian-Canadians are Canadians and there is no danger that Canada or its dominant culture will be dismissed from their lives. On the contrary, the danger of loss, Paci argues, is all on the other side of the cultural duality. What Paci shows are the costs on all levels of abandoning the past, denying the body and the blood, and of trying to live without reference to both worlds. This cost is borne primarily by the older generation but not exclusively so. Both Joey and Marie are psychologically scarred just like the old Italian neighbourhood of the West End. Generational "progress" into dominant culture, like urban renewal, may be inevitable, but it is not necessarily or entirely positive. Joey's gesture of the pyramid, like Marie's projected return to Italy, and Annalise's return to the Sault from Toronto and

New York are thus important statements in the novel in that they affirm the value of what is lost in the process, and what can be retained from that past and what can be achieved in the future.

It is in this sense that Paci's writing, like that of Atwood, constitutes a process of evaluation of general Canadian culture (as seen through the filter of Italian-Canadian experience) and a commentary on Canadian place, Canadian values and indeed universal values in general. As noted earlier, Paci's interests are multiple and his discussions of, for example, the material and the spiritual, the heart and the mind, hockey and art, family dynamics and other issues clearly do provide a broader commentary on the Canadian scene and life in general. Indeed, in a scene which eerily echoes the setting and spirit world experiments of Joan Foster in *Lady Oracle*, Marie's final reconciliation with her mother takes place in the parents' darkened bedroom with Marie "transfixed" and staring into a mirror, candles lit in the background. It is at this point that her mind "unloosens", she feels "her mother's presence in the room", she utters her apology "Mamma, I'm sorry" (192), and sees her mother's face "soften," "restored" and smiling. Clearly, Paci, like Atwood, is very much at home in the "underground" world of psychological space and his message of reconciliation of mind and body, present and past is no less universal and interesting than that of Atwood. At the same time, Paci's exploration of these issues remain informed by the particular dilemmas and dichotomies which agitate his principal characters and his ethnic minority perspective in the novel gives a unique angle on these broader aspects of Canada and human experience in general.

In both *Lady Oracle* and *Black Madonna*, Canada and Italy are juxtaposed in a variety of contexts that comment on individual psychology, family dynamics, Canadian culture and society. For Atwood, the "otherness" of immigrants and foreign space (Italy) provides a means of exploring British-Canadian mainstream gender issues and culture as well as the universal dynamics of the psyche as she sees it. Paci's world view is no less philosophical, psychological and social. In *Black Madonna* as elsewhere in his writing, he addresses philosophical and theological questions of body and spirit, issues of sibling psychology, of generational conflict and continuity, and of the relationship of art and form. At the same time, his work *is* informed by the particular perspective he brings from his own and his shared ethnic minority experience. The particular language problems his fictional families struggle with, the gender and generational issues, the relationship of his characters to their communities and to the larger dominant Canadian culture, all these and other aspects of Paci's works are informed by his attempt to "dig deep in his own self" and to "come to terms with his Italian background." In all his novels, Paci's world is Catholic, it is Italian transplanted to the specific Canadian settings of Sault Ste. Marie or Toronto and it is Canadianized, modernized, and often in sharp contrast to the Old World poor rural lifestyle that lies in the past. The situations of Paci's characters, like the two very different brothers in *The Father*, or their two different parents, reflect from the inside the dilemmas of living with, and adjusting to, two differing cultural worlds – the Italy of before and the Canada of now. This process of adaptation, of moving between two worlds, and finding a place within them, is for Paci, a serious issue. Some characters fail – Stephen's father, Marie's mother – and are destroyed in the process. The young, on the other hand, are on a continual search for understanding, for values, for emotional relationships, for place, and are crippled or successful (or both) in the course of this search. Almost always, there is generational conflict, a battle of values and identity on the differing assumptions of Canadian and Italian worlds. In this dynamic, it is safe to conclude that for Paci, Italy will always remain more significant than it could ever be for Atwood. At the same time, it is also no less true that the particular perspective on Canada and the general issues that arise from Paci's works remain no less revealing.

WORKS CITED

Atwood, Margaret. *Lady Oracle*. Toronto: McClelland and Stewart, 1976. Seal Edition, 1977.

Edwards, Caterina. *The Lion's Mouth*. Edmonton: NeWest Press, 1982.

Micone, Marco. *Déjà l'agonie*. Montreal: L'Hexagone, 1988.

Minni, C.D. "An Interview with Frank G. Paci." *Canadian Literature* 106 (1985): 5-15.

——. *Other Selves*. Montreal: Guernica Editions, 1985.

Paci, F.G. *Black Madonna*. Ottawa: Oberon, 1982.

——. *The Italians*. Ottawa: Oberon, 1978.

——. *The Father*. Ottawa: Oberon, 1984.

——. "Tasks of the Canadian Novelist Writing on Immigrant Themes." *Contrasts: Comparative Essays on Italian-Canadian Writing*. Ed. J. Pivato. Montreal: Guernica Editions, 1985. 35-60.

Wurst, Gayle. "Cultural Stereotypes and the Language of Identity: Margaret Atwood's *Lady Oracle*, Maxine Hong Kingston's *The Woman Warrior* and Alice Walker's *The Color Purple*." *Cross-Cultural Studies: American, Canadian and European Literatures*, 1945-1985. Ed. Mirko Jurak. Ljubljana, Yugoslavia: University of Ljubljana, 1988. 53-64.

"THE MOST SACRED AND SECRET THINGS OF LIFE"

Religious Imagery in the Writings of Frank Paci

ANNA CARLEVARIS

What is notable in the work of Frank Paci, whose novels are genealogically linked, forming an extended family tree, is the recurring use of religious imagery in both its sacred and prosaic aspects. At times religious custom is presented through hallucinatory episodes, at other times it becomes folklorist description of Italian immigrant life. Yet it is this very ambiguity, which both respects and mocks the high drama of Roman Catholicism, that enables Paci to explore religious practice from both the outside and the inside. As an outsider, personified as the ex-seminarian, born-again pagan Patrick Murphy of *Sex and Character* (1993), the damage caused by The Church on individual freedom and personal growth is seen as severe and irreparable. From Murphy's perspective, modern religions have become stale and sentimentalized, destructive not only to the human spirit but to society at large. Murphy's attempted suicide, after a series of hedonistic experiments in Toronto's Yorkville of the 1960s, is seen as a consequence of the

Church's inability to keep in step with the times and satisfy the spiritual hunger of its youth. From this same vantage point Lorianna in *The Italians* (1978) is also seen as a victim of historical religions' failure to address modern concerns. She is able to endure her husband's cruelty only at the expense of cutting off her own feelings and escaping into an imagined world of angels, saints and martyrs, where she exists in a kind of delirious rapture. Her detachment from reality and her recurrent, religiously-framed visions describe the essence of traumatic experience, a catalepsy Paci suggests is tacitly sustained by the Church's inadequate response to issues of gender inequality.

> The Sisters had instructed her well. No matter how the body was abused by others, as they had so often told her, it was the will that counted. If one didn't submit in will, one was still pure inside. She had felt little of that purity at first.
>
> *Italians,* 52

However, there is also Paci the insider, who as a writer understands the language and singular imagery of Catholicism as a complex system of signs, metaphors and paradox. It is this latter Paci, who in the context of post-modernity and post-structuralist thought, offers the reader a view of Catholicism that goes beyond conventional sociological critique to an exploration of its semantics and syntax to reveal a vocabulary of expressive depth and evocative imagery. The complexity of Catholic iconography makes it appropriate to the distressed field of post-modernity where writers and artists revel in multiplicity, fragmentation and in the instrumentality of the body as the mediator of knowledge and the archive of memory. Its excesses seem to intersect contemporary artistic expression at various junctures, formally, in the use of allegory and thematically in ideas of mortality, physical suffering, and spiritual redemption. By situating the themes and motifs of Catholicism within contemporary social and cultural circumstance – which includes sexuality, illness, and gender – the figurative effect of its imagery is heightened rather than diminished and its power as representation amplified. These same tendencies have led writers such as Paci to appropriate and reevaluate traditional religious imagery and concepts in order to test the boundaries of common experience.

Within a larger field of activity that includes not only creative writers but cultural theorists and visual artists as well, Paci's baroque indulgence – bloody visions of a crucified Christ, scenes of fevered carnal temptation – become explorations of what has been coined "threshold" experience. Paci recognizes in the dramaturgical or performative nature of Catholicism what anthropologist Victor Turner in his studies of ritual identifies as "liminality," an ambiguous space between social and personal order, that functions as a kind of anti-structure to the everyday world. Concepts of time, materiality and social identity dissolve in the arena of the sacred where paradox abounds, no more so than in the sacrament of the Eucharist and the miracle of Transubstantiation where the Eucharistic wafer becomes both signifier and referent, that is, both a sign of Christ's presence and Christ's actual presence. In *The Italians* Lorianna's older brother Aldo, who is studying to become a priest, recalls the awe with which he witnessed the Eucharist's transformation when he was a child – "The body was there visibly present, tangible, Godly and vulnerable at its side, where the centurion's spear was to penetrate" (57). The rituals of the Mass appear to the young Aldo as something close to a magical conjuring act – "Ever since he could remember, he wanted to have the privilege of doing the wondrous things that only a priest was capable of doing ... the power of changing the bread and wine into the body and blood of Christ" (57). It is through ritual re-enactment and its distinct spaces, instruments, words and sounds, that the power of the sacred is made manifest. Rituals make new realities appear but also dissolve them; they are repetitive acts that dispel diachronic order, create anti-time or what Walter Benjamin has called "messianic time," the collapse of past and future into an all-encompassing now. This concept of time is different from "immigrant time" where the present and future is swallowed by the gaping wound produced by a past that can no longer be retrieved – the daily burden of memory and failed ambitions. By braiding sacred and secular time together, Paci expands the inadequate contours of daily life so that it may contain the mythic as well as the mundane.

The crucified Christ has been an especially potent image to artists and to Paci as well because of the

inevitability of human mortality, the acknow-
ledgment that mortification of the body is fundamental to spiritual fulfillment. It is in this sense that Paci's
sensibility may be described as baroque, for he is
much aware of the dialectical contest between the
senses and the spirit, the tension that produces the
"black blood" that stains the pages of the sacred.
Perhaps the single most compelling image Paci has
created of this struggle between spirit and matter is
the attempted suicide scene in *Sex and Character*, the
tragic close to Murphy's avaricious attempts at personal salvation. Murphy, on a bad acid trip, returns
to St. Michael's College chapel to colour its walls and
altar in his own blood. A pale, naked and bloody
body, Murphy lies in the arms of a shocked and
speechless Mark Trecroci, the story's protagonist, the
two forming a modern day Pietà.

> Yes, I said to myself. The body and blood changed back,
> as if our lives were recoiling from the original rites. The
> body and blood transformed into bread and wine to feed
> the masses their hungry bodies.
>
> *Sex and Character*, 190-191

It is moments such as this that suggest the notion of
liminality, the meeting point between two worlds, the
space of metaphor, the transformative illuminating
instant of understanding that is beyond articulation.

Paci's references to the philosophy of Wittgenstein, suggest that the mind may not be able to
comprehend the place beyond language, the sound-
less space across which individuals communicate that

is impervious to analysis. Ironically, this intellectual realization is continually confronted by Mark's relentless, almost physical, need to speak and to write:

> I could feel it in my bones, in my blood – that it was the language that would reveal to me the most sacred and secret things of life. But at the same time, I had no way of testing whether the message carried by language was true, or even authentic.
>
> *Sex and Character,* 64

For Mark, a theological student at Saint Michael's, English is the language of the intellect and comes to represent his individuality as a grown man but it is also the language of his passion, the books he inhabits as if they were women's bodies. Trapped between his professional world and his blue collar immigrant upbringing, language also marks the cultural fissures that dominate his life. Mark's continual effort to resolve the deep divisions of his experience as a twice-removed displaced immigrant (from northern Ontario to the metropolis Toronto) finds a temporary resolution in moments of wordlessness. When Mark returns to his family in Sault Ste. Marie, he visits a site with aboriginal pictographs in order to view the language of pre-history, the human world before writing. For Paci Catholic imagery is a similar type of "elemental" language that precedes the restrictions of historical contingency and logic; it shares with ancient pictographs the power of the image. Mark's return to his childhood garden is, in Lacanian psychoanalytic terms, a return to a pre-linguistic wholeness.

Although the garden may be interpreted as a sanctu-
ary, an oasis within a hostile environment – as is St.
Mike's to the surrounding city of Toronto – in the
context of Paci's religious thematics it is closer to the
idea of the Garden of Eden. The return to the Garden
at the end of *Sex and Character* signals a return to
Origin, the end of one cycle and the start of a new
one.

Paci's characters live anguished lives, caught between extremes: desire and duty, physical and intellectual labour, city and hinterland, old and new
world, masculine and feminine forces. These dichotomies are abundant and wrestled with relentlessly, and
they form the viscous fluid of torment, the "black
blood," that courses through Paci's stories. It is the
black bile of the sanguine personality type, melan-
cholic and unconsolable that describes many of Paci's
characters. It is an inherited contamination of the
spirit, a confusion of identity that is both particular
to immigrant life as well as to the post-modern Subject. Although the pressure to choose a definitive
identity –Canadian or Italian – is on a significant level
a cultural reality tied to immigrant experience, Paci
manages to retain a larger field of vision that refuses
to limit itself to historical forces. Thus fable, myth,
sacred liturgy become the vehicles for overcoming
history, the sheer weight of material existence and
loss that envelopes the first-generation immigrant and
from which the second generation yearns to escape.
Nevertheless, from out of these dark waters of generational conflict emerge the transformative mo-

ments of insight. These occur when the dualities of experience on both personal and social levels find temporary coherence, that is, when metaphor happens, as in the delicate equilibrium represented by the garden.

Paci's characters are haunted by religion in the way that childhood memories return unbidden, incomplete and resonant in their effect. Bleeding hearts, dark fragrant spaces, luminous coloured glass, angels with flaming swords, organ music. They establish a syntax for suffering that is nevertheless stunning in its many aspects. A steel smelter is changed into purgatory, a hospital room into Gethsemane, a misunderstood brother into St. Sebastian, the inevitability of sacrifice prophesied in the family name Trecroci (three crosses). Even as many lapsed Catholics dismiss its practice or beliefs the iconography remains powerful because it is learned during childhood and thus remains rooted in memory. In Paci's work, the sensual excess of pre-Vatican II maintains a steady hold on his imagination and nourishes his creativity. As anachronistic and stereotypical as they may appear, these images intercept memory and stimulate conflicting emotions; as over determined signs, their meanings expand and multiply uncontrollably. But because they are partial recollections seen as through a child's eyes they retain the sense of the fabulous. The literal understanding with which children receive biblical narrative, the astonishment with which the magic of church ritual is confronted is distinct from the pedantic application of Church rule and law which many adults have assumed religion to be. Paci is able to recall this wonder on occasion when, in *The Father* (1984), Stephen reenacts the children's story of "Marcellino Pane e Vino" – the boy to whom a crucifix came to life (21-23).

The narrative form of scripture and its familial terms of references has made Christian doctrine easily accessible but the simplicity of its exposition has also contributed to a confusion between sacred and social order, a willingness to emulate its hierarchical trappings and a too easy fascination with the materiality of its customs. This is what Murphy complains of as the "Italian love of pomp and circumstance no matter how irrelevant." On a psychological level the conflation between religious symbolism and socially determined reality has, in the case of Lorianna, rendered her unable to live to her full potential. When we are first introduced to Lorianna at her wedding her conflicted fantasy life is immediately revealed to us when the accordions in the banquet hall become to her the sound of cathedral organ music. Her incapacity to integrate her religious upbringing, and previous ambition to be a nun, with her actual life as an individual – woman – wife, leads to a disastrous start to married life.

And yet, even as the rituals of Catholicism appear at times to be all smoke and mirrors they also feed the imagination through the power of metaphor and allegorical narrative. For to see one's life reflected in the otherworldly is to partake in myth and, ultimately, to transcend time and the drudgery of earthly existence. When Margaret Laurence counsels the young writer Mark she encourages him to "write about your Italian background where the world began for you" (180). Paci, the writer, ritually returns to this "Italian background," to the same characters and locations although their names may change. But ultimately, "where the world begins" for Paci is a place before and after all things, the sacred space of his "beautiful garden."

WORKS CITED

Benjamin, Walter. *Illuminations*. New York: Schocken, 1970.

Lacan, Jacques. *Speech and Language in Psychoanalysis*. Trans. A. G. Wilden. Baltimore: The Johns Hopkins Press, 1982.

Paci, F.G. *The Italians*. Ottawa: Oberon Press, 1978.

_____. *The Father*. Ottawa: Oberon Press, 1984.

_____. *Black Blood*. Ottawa: Oberon Press, 1991.

_____. *Sex and Character*. Ottawa: Oberon Press, 1993.

PROVISIONALITY, MULTIPLICITY
AND THE IRONIES OF IDENTITY IN
Black Madonna

MARINO TUZI

Frank Paci's *Black Madonna* conveys a markedly ambiguous view of the Italian Canadian experience. The conclusion of the novel is equivocal since closure and resolution are coexistent with a sense of flux and change. Although the central characters, Joey and Marie Barone, momentarily resolve a crisis of identity by reincorporating their Italian heritage into a Canadian perspective, transformation remains incomplete and unstable.

The text examines the tentativeness and heterogeneity of Italian Canadianness, refuting any notion of a singular and coherent subjectivity. It also asserts that ethnicity is socially constructed. Joey and Marie are shown to be participating in the evolution of their self-images through a set of choices which demonstrate to them the arbitrariness of competing cultural models.

Irony is critical to the way the text fashions its discourse on identity formation. According to Frank Paci, "The task of the novelist, then, is to create a proper tension between what to say and what not to say"(54). The foregrounding of the opposing values and confused thoughts and actions of the characters is invested with paradox. Irony arises out of the omniscient narrator's mediation between the consciousness of the characters and the external world. It is also built into the plot structure and image patterns of the text.

The complexities of adjustment are enacted through Joey's and Marie's distinct but thematically linked focalizations. In both narratives the conjoining and reforming of vantage points is exemplified by the friction between Italian and English and by the co-presence of the languages.

Equally important, the juxtaposition of discordant cultural images stresses the central characters' ambivalence towards two divergent social orders. The uncertainties of identity formation, as dramatized through the varied experiences of the two protagonists leads the ethnic subject "to cultivate a sophisticated capacity for ambiguity, juxtaposition, and irony" (Hutcheon, 52). These representational strategies are supported by the use of symbolism and imagery which emanate from references to aspects of Italian immigrant culture and mainstream society. Symbols and images are endowed with a multitude of overlapping and conflicting meanings in order to emphasize the intricacies and discontinuities of ethnicity. Accompanying this formal strategy is the motif of role-playing which suggests that the identities of the Italian-descended protagonists are socially produced and composed of a diversity of subject-positions.

Eli Mandel notes that John Marlyn's *Under the Ribs of Death* (1956) relies on the ironies of plot in its depiction of the Hungarian Canadian (11). Elsewhere Linda Hutcheon observes that frequently "the ironies [of being ethnic] are less verbal than structural: such as the larger narrative ironies surrounding the character Marie in Frank Paci's *Black Madonna*"(57). While making salient the idea of difference, irony also is inclusive: ethnic identity contests and accommodates a spectrum of cultural suppositions. Irony presents an "awareness of contingency and multiplicity" (56-57), and "questions the very act" and authority "of taking a position, any position, even an oppositional one" (*Open Letter*, 69). Irony announces "an unwillingness to make decisions about meaning that would imply singularity or fixity" and disputes any "fixed, authoritative meaning" (69-70). In minority texts, such as *Black Madonna*, irony envelops the indeterminacy and disjunctions of the ethnic subject. Linda Hutcheon surmises that in ethnic writing "irony is at least potential in . . . anything problematic or relative" (*Splitting*, 52).

1. The Ironies of Identity Formation

The narrative of Joey Barone depends on a series of ironies which comment on the precariousness of identity formation. The death of his father, Adamo, and the attendant collapse of his mother, Assunta, which force him to take over the household and reframe his point of reference, inaugurate the protagonist's reappraisal of the cultural assumptions which have guided his behaviour. Joey is appalled by Assunta's ritualistic self-effacement and believes that Adamo's struggles in Canada have been in vain. Actions and their meanings appear suddenly to be provisional: "And he knew how fragile everything else was . . . The membrane between being and non-being was so thin he could feel the cold wind blow through it and chill his spine" (*Black Madonna*, 53).

The questioning of previous decisions such as giving up the possibility of a hockey career and following in his father's footsteps strengthens his relationship with his girlfriend, Annalise, putting his personal needs before his obligation to his mother. Although his parents had provided a secure domestic environment, their resistance (especially in his mother's case) to Canadianization hampered his development. This interrogation of ethnicity, in which Joey wants to divest himself of its objectionable elements, results in a confirmation of its power. Yet the narrative's redemptive moments – Joey's reconciliation with his sister and the erecting of a brick pyramid that is a totem to the immigrant past –are infused with a sense of flux.

Marie's story is also governed by a set of structural ironies. The paradox of the flight from Little Italy becomes apparent to her after she understands that her marriage is as burdensome as her Italian family: "She was a wife and a mother now – a mere woman who had to fulfil her biological requirements" (143).

In order to support her husband in graduate school and their young son, Marie accepts work as a high-school teacher, thus relinquishing her post-graduate studies in mathematics. Through her academic ambitions, she had tried to sever the connection to a part of her personal history which, in raising her son, she now observes, is no longer alien to her.

Marie had repudiated Assunta's domineering maternalism, but she herself is overprotective and intolerant towards her son's behaviour: she reprimands him for refusing to eat her nutritious meal. Despite Marie's choice of a way of life (a choice of life that is different from Assunta's), she is endowed with some of her mother's characteristics.

Similarly, while Joey secretly dreamed of becoming something other than a labourer in the local steel mill, his familial duty, his manual dexterity, and his lack of impetuosity illustrate Adamo's deep-seated influence.

Marie's emotional outpouring at Assunta's funeral frees her and enables her to rejoin the broken circuits of her ethnicity. Structurally and emotionally, her decision to leave her immigrant culture is supplanted by a circular movement back to her origins. The images of the black dress which her mother wore and the Hope Chest containing Assunta's modest dowry are emblematic of Italian femininity. Marie's varying responses to these artifacts imply a shift in perspective. Before becoming disenchanted with mainstream society, Marie had viewed the donning of a black dress and the use of the Hope Chest as signs of a backward culture. Ironically, these very items will allow Marie to reconstitute her lost matrilinearity. They invoke the re-emergence of her ethnicity. Emaciated, Marie in a black dress at her mother's funeral connects with her mother when Marie discovers in the Hope Chest a picture of a young, thin Assunta. This physical resemblance reveals the spiritual link between mother and daughter.

Later in Assunta's room, Marie lights candles and sets up an improvised shrine to her mother's memory. Like Joey's pyramid, this reliquary, a testament to Assunta's way of life, allows Marie to rehabilitate her discarded Italianness. These images of Marie's participation in a ritual for the dead as well as her visualization of her mother's ghostly presence are in sharp contrast to her past denigration of emotion and superstition.

2. Double Narration

Told in the third person and organized into numerous episodes, the events in the novel unfold through the individual perspectives of Joey and Marie Barone. The first unit of the text presents Joey's point of view and accentuates the schism between brother and sister. Joey is concerned about his mother's mental state after the death of his father and Marie decries Assunta's archaic practices. Marie abandons her mother to her brother's care and resumes her routine in Toronto.

The ambiguity of Marie's facial expression, captured in the statement that Joey "couldn't tell whether she was pitying him or asking for his forgiveness" (10), prefigures the alternation between Joey and Marie's story. Each character breaks away from Italian culture, and this thematic link highlights the problematic nature of ethnicity. The stylistic variance between the two narratives reveals differing reactions to this crisis of identity. The brother's story occurs predominantly in present time. It spans a critical year in his development, and is interspersed with occasional flashbacks to his youth. The movement of the seasons which accompanies the passing of the first generation – Adamo's funeral in the winter, and of Assunta's decline in the spring and of her death in the summer – implies that transformation is certain and traumatic. By concluding Joey's narrative in late summer and not in the fall, which would have completed the representation of the seasonal cycle, the text points to an open-ended process. The coming of fall marks another stage in Joey's personal evolution.

In contrast, Marie's narrative moves from the past (her adolescence) to the present (her life as a single parent). This longer time frame which begins in spring and ends in summer is archetypally suggestive of birth and maturity but is laden with ambiguity. Marie's rebellion against Assunta and the shakiness of her marriage are counterbalanced by her reconciliation with her Italian heritage and her growing sense of independence.

The discrepancy in time frame between the main

two stories of the novel emphasizes the distinctiveness of Marie and Joey's psychological journey. The juxtaposition of Joey's story (present time) to that of Marie (the past) implies that anxiety and transformation are inevitable. Present time in Joey's narrative makes immediate the conflict between individuality and filial duty. The linear movement of Marie's story, from past to present, shows a progressive disengagement from family and assimilation into the mainstream.

This double narrative describing the divergent histories of brother and sister is the prism through which is refracted a variety of subject-positions. Both sister and brother are simultaneously inside and outside their social milieux and, by implication, their Canadian and Italian identities. As the last quarter of the novel attests, while Marie slowly reclaims her Italian culture, Joey is ready to leave his parents' home, having arrived at his independence through his relationship with Annalise, a member of mainstream society. Each episode begins in present time – Marie's disappointment with her marriage and Joey's bewilderment towards Assunta – and then switches to the past: Marie remembers her relationship with Richard; Joey listens to Father Sarlo who furnishes him with a brief historical sketch of the Italian community. Both narratives return to and conclude in the present – where the text gives Marie and Joey's reasons for failure in Little Italy and mainstream society.

The variation in speech patterns (conspicuous in

the dialogue between brother and sister, and in their internal monologues) ostensibly demarcates antithetical social positions. Such polarization is weakened by the unmistakable similarities in the characters' multiple language systems. Marie's language has been formed by her university education and profession. Her ability with words is integral to the way she bestows meaning on experience. Marie employs figurative language when she describes her mother's past behaviour: "The [kitchen] table was like [Assunta's] theatre of operations and her rules were unquestioned" (32). Marie also makes constant use of casual words, such as "crazy" (138) and "kids" (147). The use of casual language indicates her working-class roots and so places Marie at the same social level as her brother. However, Joey's speech is predominantly that of the everyday: it relies on the idiom and vocabulary of the working person: "Horsing around. Talking about nothing in particular . . . Then going to Tony's and shooting a few" (22). Joey incorporates in his utterance snatches of the Marchigiano dialect, exhibiting an affiliation with his ethnicity.

Another feature of both narratives is the recurrence of Italian words which helps to situate the problem of intergenerational communication and the opposition of value systems. Marie and Joey's ineptness in expressing themselves through their Italian dialect inhibits an understanding of their parents' customs and beliefs. The juxtaposing of Italian and English accentuates the ideological gap between parent and child, implying that each side is imprisoned by a form of ethnocentricism. This linguistic contrast usually occurs at critical instants, such as when Marie decides to leave home and to go to university or when Joey is shocked by Assunta's grieving.

The coexistence of the two languages is also emblematic of the overlaying of multiple viewpoints. When Joey uses his Italian dialect, he admits that his facility is poor and that he must use English to communicate with his mother. Ironically, Marie who, despite her refusal to openly speak Italian, is not only much more fluent in her native language than Joey but frequently thinks, talks, and makes references in Italian: "They were words she didn't realize she knew. '*Dove la chiave del bavulo, Mamma?*' Where is the key to the trunk?" (108)

Marie proclaims an allegiance to English mainstream culture by taking on an English name. As a young woman, she modifies her original name, Maria and, later as an adult, drops the "e" off Barone, her family name. All phonetic traces of her Italianness are thus removed. Throughout the novel, Joey is known by his English Canadian moniker.

This act of renaming recurs in Paci's works. In *The Italians* (1978), Guglielmo Gaetano becomes Bill Gaetano. In *The Father* (1984), Stefano Mancuso changes his first name to Stephen. Often linguistic alienation is not the cause, but the symptom of a collision of values for both parents and children who have grown apart from each other. In referring to Marie and Joey by their English names, the text underlines the indeterminacy of the ethnic subject, of living both within and outside various cultural contexts. The deterritorialized Italian language is recovered only when Marie and Joey reclaim their Italian heritage. Speaking overseas to their aunt, Assunta's sister (an Italian woman whom they have never met), in a language which they had considered to be childish and ineffectual, they experience a cultural affinity for the first time in their lives. By keeping their anglicized first name, Marie and Joey manifest an attachment to English Canadian society, as do Bill Gaetano and Stephen Mancuso

Further complicating the language field of each story line is the intermixing of the narrator's voice with that of the two characters. The presentation of Joey's thoughts is couched in words which often do not match his speech and which resemble Marie's use of formal English. The narrator constantly mediates Joey's perceptions, for example his view of Father Sarlo: "When the Italian priest was transferred to the parish, he was the scourge of the neighbourhood, railing against sin and stinginess with a fierceness Joey had never seen in a human being since" (146). The style, syntax, and diction of this sentence will appear in Marie's reflection on her own difficult pregnancy: "And when Michael was born, the terror of the delivery almost killing her, she was overcome with the sheer living phenomenon of him that she lost all interest in her doctoral program" (141). The imbrication of various language types indicates the overlapping of irreconcilable and complementary subject positions, which includes that of the narrator. The stylistic technique of separating and joining the voices of the two characters transmits the diversity of the ethnic subject. This motif is consolidated at the conclusion of the novel. Near the end of the text, Joey and Marie's consciousness converge and become part of the same story line. Yet, in the last episode, the voices of the two characters diverge, for we are only presented with Joey's perspective.

Each story interacts with the narrative of the immigrant experience and adds to the complexity of the protagonists' cultural positioning. In Joey's text, Father Sarlo's discussion of the cultural make-up of the first generation and of the problems of adjustment brings together two dissimilar but intersecting journeys in the new world: those of the parents and their Canadianized children. Joey obtains an overview of the efforts of Italians to retain their beliefs and customs. The novel outlines the settlement and dispersal of Little Italy in the Sault and describes the social isolation and the working conditions of the immigrant. Allusions are made to class divisions, based on economic status and ethnicity (a great many of the employees at the steel mill are Italian or of Italian descent), and to the issue of assimilation.

The transition from marginality to an acceptance of multiplicity is implied in the melding of Marie's narrative with that of the immigrant. Studying the faded photographs of her mother and extended family in the old country, Marie sees a group of individuals coping, almost heroically, with difficult circumstances: "[The land] was hilly, with every piece . . . used for cultivation . . . she saw the kind of people she came from . . . Peasants . . . trying to eke an existence from the soil" (194). Father Sarlo's account and the collection of photographs, which oppose the adult children's interpretation of their parents' behaviour, do not romanticize the past, but legitimate a devalued agrarian and working-class culture.

3. *The Use of Juxtaposition*

The perspectival ambiguity of the protagonist is developed through the use of juxtaposition. From Joey's vantage point, images of the black madonnas (including Assunta) in their hypnotic mourning ritual, the strangeness of Adamo's desiccated corpse lying on his bed, and the verbal inarticulateness of Assunta communicate a world that defies comprehension. In contrast to this confusion and bewilderment, there are images of a stable and coherent ethnic social environment. Joey is immersed in his work at the steel plant which pushes him to his limits. The domestic partnership with Adamo and Assunta entails constant renovation and household chores. Joey's passion for hockey demands a physicality which repeats the immigrant's valorization of human labour. His verbal reticence, motivated as it is by the belief that words cannot describe feelings or illuminate personal experience, privileges the intuitive over the rational. Juxtaposition constantly illustrates how Joey moves in and out of several cultural identities.

He is unsure about mainstream society, which is
represented through images of urbanism, industrialization, and technology. The novel makes brief references to the density and uniformity of city dwellings,
the clamorous and smoky steel plant, and the television set that Assunta watches surpasses time and
space. This imagery is contrasted to the game of
hockey which, for Joey, is the pre-eminent signifier
of Canadianness: "hockey was hockey, pure and simple – the only thing Canadians did the best in all the
world" (46). Uninterested in fame and fortune, Joey
plays hockey as a means of defining himself and his
relations to others. The importance of hockey is
stressed through a recurrent dream: Joey sees himself
gliding euphorically over a radiant, frozen lake. Emblematic of his desire for a state of unity, this visionary
moment is reified in Annalise's art near the end of the
novel: "[The painting] showed the side view of a
hockey player with a close resemblance to Joey skat-
ing all alone over a large expanse of ice in the out-
doors" (196). The dream imagery underscores the
protagonist's contradictory urges: the need to flee the
stifling protectiveness of home and the constraints of
a working-class, one-industry town; to make creative
use of his manual skills; to overcome the fear of living
"in the world outside the West End" (88). Hockey
permits a temporary reprieve from the psychological
desolation of his immigrant and working-class sur-
roundings: "Only when he played hockey did he feel
alive as before" (59).

While the steel mill is the source of his livelihood,

Joey finds his work arduous and unfullfilling. The futility of his labour exacerbates his helplessness and lack of direction. On the ice, Joey can extirpate his lingering boyish dependence: "He would play as if [Annalise] were the only one watching. He would play fatherless and motherless" (86). Yet the game of hockey is tarnished by greed – evident in Donny Belsito's account of its crass commercialism. It also breeds violence, as shown in the description of the steel plant hockey players who vent their personal frustrations and through the screams of blood-thirsty fans. Ironically, hockey is wedded to Italian culture. It demands the same stamina and dexterity as brick-laying or carpentry – these are trades which the protagonist learns under his father's diligent tutelage. The hockey stick is as familiar to Joey's touch as a bricklayer's trowel. ("The grain of wood had been smoothed down by such long use that it fit the contours of the palm perfectly" (63).) The opaque-ness of daily life and the vain attempts at harmonizing antagonistic cultural viewpoints are juxtaposed to the transparency of playing hockey. When thought, feel-ing, and action are integrated, time and space are transcended. ("Hockey seemed to empty him inside. There was no innerness. He was no more and no less than what he did" (59).) Countering this picture of stability are nightmare images evoking uncertainty, abandonment, menace, and death. They conflate eerie allusions to the new world – whether they are of nature or of hockey – with the immigrant commu-nity, represented by the spectral figure of a worker.

The unsettling imagery is repeated in the depiction of the steel mill as a powerful and monstrous force: "Gigantic hooks the size of a sidewalk held the pot secure just a few feet from the top . . . The light from the molten steel was so intense no-one could look at it without dark glasses. Soon the mould was filled. They stood on rail tops in the pit like a chain of miniature volcanoes, their tops glowing with white heat" (57-58). The process of steel making, wherein raw material is melted down and then recast into a particular form, is emblematic of the Italians' adaptation to a technological environment. Industrialization based on mechanization and the specialization of work modifies the immigrant's labour, directing him to a specific set of tasks. Adamo Barone had apprenticed as a bricklayer in Italy with the intent of becoming a tradesman, not just a tiny cog in a production line, "a bricklayer going to the various furnaces to line them with fire-brick. Keeping the inferno going. Instead of building homes and bridges as he had always meant to" (63).

The juxtaposing of hell's fire to old world craftsmanship implies a conflict between modern industry and immigrant aspiration. The price that the worker pays is dramatized through Adamo Barone's death which is the result of physical exhaustion and chemical toxicity. The juxtaposition of a multitude of cultural images obscures the opposition between rural and technological society. The inhospitable terrain of the home village, with its hills and rocky fields, is joined to a polluted and noisy industrial city and its surrounding wilderness. Despite the rigors of adjustment, Adamo and Assunta Barone exchange subsistence farming for a measure of economic security. Urbanism's emphasis on competition, as shown in the intellectual rivalry between Marie and Richard, and its patriarchal-based social system, which, like the patriarchal pattern of the Italian village, puts responsibility for child-rearing on the woman to the detriment of professional achievement, is as onerous as industrialization or agrarianism. The novel suggests that underneath the perceived differences between the immigrant community and mainstream society, there is a kind of interchangeability of the role of the woman.

4. *Cultural Imagery and Symbolism*

Black Madonna employs images and symbols which arise from an immigrant milieu and the cultural and mythic structures of both the old and new world. According to Paci, "The writer can't be too self-conscious in choosing images and symbols. They must already 'be there' so to speak – or be organically part of the story" (1985, 57). The symbolism and imagery are notably open-ended. The trunk in the novel generates a host of significations. It is Assunta's affiliation with her matrifocal heritage and her dowry-making for her daughter; Marie's rite of passage from ignorance to knowledge, as well as her initiation into a form of matrilinearity; an antiquated cultural practice and the disappearance of a way of life. The trunk's numerous meanings depend on the subjectivity of Marie Barone as she interchangeably rejects, reassumes, and reworks her Italian identity. The death of Adamo and Assunta represents ambiguity. The loss is tragic: it uproots Joey and Marie from their immigrant origins. Yet death liberates them by allowing them to recreate their identities. The allusions to Italian history and culture are contiguous with images of the mainstream (hockey, the natural landscape, industrialization, and urbanism). These allusions and images serve a symbolic function and their meanings change according to the shifting point of view of the central characters. Annalise's paintings imbue the banalities of the everyday with a sense of wonder: she tells Joey, "I want to have people see what they see as if for the first time. The marvel of it" (163).

The text's rendering of the immigrant community and Canadian society commingles realism with melodrama, myth, and folklore. Pre-Christian and Christian mythology recurs in the novel, mainly through the presence of Assunta, who personifies the Black Madonna figure. Assunta's nurturing qualities, marked by her corpulence, physicality and closeness to the soil, are contrasted to her mourning rituals and self-abnegation. Contrary attributes make her the Great Goddess of female mythology. In an article on *Black Madonna*, Roberta Sciff-Zamaro indicates that Assunta is "the mysterious, almost sibylline character," and embodies "the primordial feminine principle in the collective unconscious" that "is almost

completely effaced" in Christian mythology (87-90).
In both Catholic Mediterranean culture and the Great
Goddess myth, the colour black refers to mortality:
"the black phase [is] connected with death and the
underworld" (90) Like the Great Goddess, Assunta is
invested with contradictory meanings creativity and
destructiveness are indistinguishable. The ambivalence of the Goddess/Madonna figure reflects the
paradoxes of immigrant culture.

Within the Italian community, the Black Madonna is an icon for the duplicities of an agrarian past
which revolve around cultivation, one's relation to
the earth, and privation, the often deadly struggle to
make a living out of a rock-hard land. The cult of the
Madonna is tied to ancient pagan beliefs which saw
the land as an embodiment of the Great Goddess and
her powers of life and death. In Roman Catholicism,
the Virgin Mary symbolizes purity, vitality, and moth-
erhood as well as suffering and mortality. In Italian
peasant culture, La Madonna speaks of fatalism, spiritual redemption, economic enslavement and moral
perseverance. The text revises this mythic figure and
comments on the internal familial conflicts of the
Italian Canadian community. As the text's overarching trope for Italianness, the "Black Madonna" is
an oxymoron: while Assunta represents the nurturer,
the virgin mother undefiled by life, she is also the
destroyer whose domineering ways threaten her adult
children's individuality.

This binarism is undermined by the contradictions
of Assunta's personal history. As a young woman she

longed for the old country, but its economic draw-
backs compelled her to seek opportunity elsewhere.
Marriage, the building of family, and the fulfilling of
the established roles of wife and mother were made
possible in the host country because of its economic
opportunities. The death of her husband shatters her
world and exposes her to what she had perceived to
be the spiritual emptiness of industrial society. Although the novel implies that she participated in her
own defeat because of her refusal to become familiar
with mainstream society, Assunta is overwhelmed by
forces beyond her control.

Her character is not just an incarnation of *La
Madonna,* as suggested by her promulgation of traditional values. Assunta is victimized in the old and new
world because she belonged to a working-class and
ethnic community. Her symbolic association to the
Great Goddess/Black Madonna figure not only de-
lineates her nurturing and authoritarian tendencies as
a mother, it also insinuates a kind of martyrdom.
Ironically, like her son and daughter, she is both part
of and estranged from her native culture. Her with-
drawal from daily life after the death of her husband
is as much a break from Italian cultural patterns as it
is an escape from the harsh realities of the new
society.

Viewed in Joey and Marie's narratives, Assunta
mostly functions as a projection of their ambivalence
towards their ethnicity. Images of Assunta frequently
express a rupture between the old and new world.
This is apparent in such images when Assunta is

draped in a black dress, her hair in disarray, sitting vacuously before the television set which sheds an eerie light around her, or when in the religious procession the "Black Madonnas [are] engulfed by the younger, more colourfully dressed women" (27). Assunta's terrible death expands the narrative's exploration of the nether side of Italian Canadianness. Yearning to return home after Adamo's death, she finds solace in the open space surrounding the railway tracks because it reminds her of the hilly fields of her youth. While crossing the railway tracks near her home, she is cut in half by a speeding, oncoming train. Industrial, technological society, evoked by the train, is essentially equivocal. Although it promises the southern Italian labourer and his family economic improvement, it exacts a terrible price. This difficult condition puts incredible assimilative pressures on the second generation. When Joey sees the carnage by the railway, he faces the full brunt of his own cultural dislocation.

5. *The Social Production of Identity*

In *Black Madonna*, the continual emphasis on cultural contexts and role-models implies that ethnicity is at the meeting point of contending social forces. Julie Beddoes' analysis of form and the process of subject formation in John Marlyn's *Under the Ribs of Death* (1957), another fictional text concerned with ethnic identity, is equally applicable to *Black Madonna*.

Beddoes contends that the fictional biography of the
protagonist, Sandor/Alex, is constructed from a diversity of "surrounding [cultural] texts" and "models of
selfhood" which appear to be discontinuous and incomplete: "Hungarianness is not portrayed as a coherent collection of attributes, or source of identity,
and neither is Englishness" (7-8). The use of irony in
the novel exposes the disjunctions and ambiguities of
the central character's multiple subject positions.

Likewise, *Black Madonna*'s ironic representation
of Italianness continuously invokes the indeterminacy
of the two protagonists' cultural positioning. In Joey's
narrative, he sees his parents primarily in terms of
their patriarchal-matrifocal roles: Adamo is the
breadwinner and Assunta is the centre of the household. They tend not only to guide Joey but to over-
protect him because they are worried about the
harmful effects of Canadian society. His mother at-
tends to his personal needs by cooking him meals and
ironing his clothes: his father teaches him his trade,
finds a job for him at the steel mill, and discourages
him from pursuing a career in hockey because Adamo
thinks it is antithetical to family values and the work
ethic. Joey's dependence on his parents is personified
by his name, a diminutive of Joseph, which indicates
that in their eyes he is always their little boy. Underneath this controlled domestic environment, there is
a simmering friction between Joey's desires and his
parents' values which is compounded at times by his
unfamiliarity with his parents' beliefs and customs.

The chaos unleashed in the aftermath of Adamo's

passing and Assunta's inconsolable grief breaks open Joey's doubts about his ethnicity. Since his Italianness is only one part of his identity, his mother no longer acts as a positive role-model but is perceived as the other who is disconnected from Canadian society. He cannot fathom Assunta's decision to have Adamo's body in the house. After Adamo's funeral, Assunta, in a numbed state, watches television interminably as the household falls into disorder. She performs a self-effacing mourning ritual, cutting "her own hair down to the skin" (82). This not only shocks Joey's Canadian sensibility but further deepens his trepidation:

> "She had never ceased to puzzle him . . . She had strange old-country customs that . . . were primitive and embarrassing" (11). Assunta's emotional and physical deterioration terrifies him and disorients him. During his father's wake, he had felt a deep love for his mother: "this frail woman [who] was closer to him than any other human being." (18)

Misinterpreting Assunta's actions as signs of mental illness, Joey brings her to a psychiatrist for rehabilitation. Assunta refuses to cooperate because she sees psychiatric treatment as a form of cultural intervention which will deny the legitimacy of her sorrow and, in effect, rob her of her traditional feminine role. The underlying social implications of such medical treatment for Assunta are beyond her son's understanding.

When he turns for assistance to Father Sarlo, the spokesman for the Italian community, we observe the extent of Joey's misreading of his mother's actions.

The priest's sympathetic analysis of the experiences of the Italian community in Sault Saint Marie operates discursively as a counterpoint to Joey's partial understanding of his ethnic group. Father Sarlo insists that the gap between the first and second generation is fundamentally social and ideological. Although the parents have retained their customs and language, the children have been Canadianized. Peasant society, perhaps technologically unsophisticated but steeped in folklore and religiosity, has equipped the immigrant with civilizing skills and ingrained in him/her a deep-seated impulse for community:

> this neighbourhood . . . was . . . where they could make a . . . village where everyone could know each other. (159)

The novel, however, hints that identification with one's social group and family does not extinguish individuality. There is a subtlety, complexity, and ambiguity to the characterization of Adamo and Assunta which implies that identity is not reducible to a set of cultural traits.

The insertion of Father Sarlo's narrative suggests that Joey's insensitivity towards Assunta's distress is not simply the outcome of an unconscious absorption of Canadian values. Instead, Joey is projecting his own despair over his cultural instability; he is torn between filial duty and his plan for independence. By mediating between the old world, embodied by family and home, and the new, represented by the steel mill, Adamo had allowed Joey to integrate momentarily parts of his identity. With the death of his father, the bridge between the two worlds has collapsed and this breakdown now exposes the son's underlying ambivalence towards his ethnicity.

Mesmerized by his mother's actions, he can see only the deadly atavisms of an immigrant culture. Older members in the Italian enclave do not deem her behaviour to be aberrant. The practiced mourners, the black madonnas, who participate at Adamo's wake, Father Sarlo, and a family friend are all sympathetic towards Assunta's demonstrations of sorrow. The death of his parents makes Joey vulnerable to the uncertainties of being Italian Canadian and forces him to rethink his cultural positioning. Even the safety of family had been precarious, given the tension between mother and daughter and the repression of Joey's own aspirations. He has coped since childhood with competing cultural attitudes. His parents' presence and his emotional and social dependency on them had created the illusion of a coherent cultural environment. As Marie brutally tells her brother,

> [Assunta]'s kept you as an emotional cripple. She's done everything for you like a true Italian Mamma, hasn't she? (161)

The text implies that Joey was complicit in insulating himself from the world.

Marie's conflictual relationship with Assunta foregrounds the opposition of gender/cultural role models. On the one hand, Assunta insists that a

woman should devote herself to the home, to being
a wife and mother. On the other, Marie asserts that
a woman should pursue a professional career and
share familial responsibilities with her partner.
Through this intergenerational strife, the reader is
made aware that femininity is a social and cultural
construction. Marie, like Joey, has to locate and assess
her identity within the structures of radically different
social orders. The communication gap between Marie
and Assunta is conveyed through a series of culturally
charged images. During the feast of Our Lady of
Mount Carmel, Marie, who is sixteen years old at the
time, refuses to go to Mass with her mother. She
considers the Church procession to be a primitive
ritual that is totally out of place in the new world.
Marie associates the image of "black-draped old
women of the parish with rosaries dangling from their
hands" (23) with that of Assunta "reciting the Hail
Marys one after another, her face dark and fervent"
(25). She finds her mother's devout expression indistinguishable from the faces of the widowed and aged
women of the community. Marie likens Assunta's
unrefined behaviour, "screaming out her name [to
come to dinner] at the top of lungs" (27) to that of "a
vulgar washerwoman" (27). This deprecating view
encompasses all the women in the neighbourhood:

> The Italian women shopping at the grocery stores, feeling
> or smelling every piece of food . . . Large Italian women
> with their dime-store dresses and huge shopping-bags pa-
> trolled the wares. (29)

To both the adolescent and adult Marie, Assunta is a fossil, a throwback to a time and place with values that are irrelevant to the modern world:

> Remaining so blatantly old-country with her vulgar ways. Like still keeping a chamber pot under her bed at night. Or yelling at the top of her voice when she was angry. Or chattering like a magpie when her friends came to visit. (39)

Although Assunta is grooming her daughter to become a wife and mother, Marie wants to be an independent woman, free from the restrictions of domesticity:

> There is more to the world, Ma, than cooking and keeping house for a man, you don't understand. A girl has to make a life for herself (73).

Marie's criticism of Assunta's ways focuses on the unadorned physicality and lack of refinement of immigrant culture. She idealizes English middle-class life, prizing what she feels is its cultural elitism and believing in its promise of self-advancement. Her relationship with Richard Charlton, a philosophy student, and their subsequent marriage reinforce her valorization of urban and technological society. Richard, like Marie, believes that personal crises can be resolved rationally by imposing order and meaning on the pell-mell of experience.

Paradoxically, Marie's interpretation of her mother's behaviour, however, betrays not just a contestation of old world beliefs but an inability to manage her Italian and Canadian identities. Unlike Joey, who stymied his individuality for the conveniences offered by family life, Marie renounces her past for the putative stability of an urban lifestyle. Her project of integration is an attempt to give coherence to her identity, for Assunta is not the primary reason for Marie's rebelliousness. Ironically, the protagonist, in denying her feminine bond with her mother, overlooks their commonality. Assunta is just as preoccupied with her appearances as Marie. The image of Assunta in a new print dress, which "was light blue, with white flowers" (25) and the "touch of lipstick" (26) on her lips during the *festa* are connected to Marie's self-consciousness about her weight and poor "complexion" (30).

The irony of Marie's perceptions of Italian culture is obvious in her family's response to her behaviour. Adamo's description of intergenerational conflict is a veiled reference to Marie's assimilation:

> "The kids move out first," Adamo said. "As soon as they get enough money to buy a house in the East End. They move away from their parents. They don't want to do with their parents anymore, hey. They become English." (66).

Joey's muted shock at Marie's condescension towards their parents demonstrates that he sees his sister as someone who looks at the family from the outside, from an English Canadian middle-class matrix. These opposing perspectives, like Father Sarlo's, offer a critique of Marie's reading of her Italian community and emphasize the importance of cultural positioning.

The narrator's mediation between Marie's consciousness and the external world underscores the ironies of inhabiting a multiple identity. In Marie's mind, the images of daily life in Little Italy, especially those which focus on the immigrant woman, summon a gender/cultural orientation that she not only disavows, but abhors. This negativity, however, is directed towards the entire community and stems from her identification with Canadian society:

> Ever since going to high school, the West End was becoming more and more intolerable to her. For some reason she found almost everything about it either obnoxious or trite (29).

The condemnation of her neighbourhood is presented in an ironic manner by the narrator. The narrator separates Marie's judgements from the description of the community and suggests that Marie's opinions spring from her cultural positioning. She preferred to attend the collegiate instead of the Catholic high school so that she could become part of the mainstream and assimilate the attitudes of that milieu. Popular magazines, and their values, which are sustained daily by the girls at her school, promote a reified kind of feminine beauty which makes Marie morbidly conscious of her bodily process:

> Menstruation . . . made her feel unclean . . . it compelled
> her to improve her outward appearance . . . she had to
> hide her uncleanliness in a bright shiny vessel (31).

In turn, obesity, for Marie, signifies a personal inadequacy inherent in the excessiveness and crudeness of immigrant culture. Obsessed with being thin, she declines to eat Assunta's bountiful meals at home, widening the rift between her and her mother. The central character's anorexia nervosa, which remains a salient feature of her adult life, is emblematic of an inarticulate wish to blot out her Italianness, so powerfully concretized in the form of her mother who threatens the consolidation of her Canadian identity. There is an ambiguity here since, as we are to discover later in the novel, Marie's thinness ironically links her with her mother, the young and wiry girl in a family photograph. As articulated through the various gender role models which are made available to Marie Barone, the surrounding social texts oppose, support, and continually interact with each other. Ethnicity and femininity are not represented as a set of cultural dichotomies but as fundamentally unstable and variegated.

The complexities of identity formation, as in the case of the binary of obesity and thinness, are reiterated in the mind and body split. This dichotomy, with its attendant self-denial, is symptomatic of a deepseated and continuing malaise. Marie uses mathematics "as a way of breaking her parental connection" (139). Academic study does not remedy her anxieties about her body and sexuality. Sections of Marie's narrative depict her as emotionally and sexually dysfunctional. Marie is aroused by scenes from a movie involving a man's physical and sexual assault of a woman and by her macabre fantasy about the putrefication of her gaunt body. These scenes are contrasted to her brother's naturalness with the opposite sex:

> Of the few women Joey had known he was always surprised by the amount of passion he could engender in them by the slightest effort on his part. (129)

Countering images of Marie's convoluted sexuality are moments of eroticism which evoke ironically Assunta's physicality and association with nature:

> [Marie] could feel her body wanting to unravel, open up, and break through in the moist, dark earth. And that her body itself was composed of this moist, dark earth that wanted to take things in and push them out renewed and engorged with life. (152)

This description is reminiscent of the exhilaration felt by Joey when he participates in physical activity. The ostensible polarization of mind and body is emblematic of the two characters' incapacity to accommodate various cultural models, and is constantly subverted by contradictory attitudes and actions. As Marie's marriage slowly falls apart, she admits that the valorizing of order and logic has deprived her of sexual fulfillment and has damaged the possibility of intimacy with her husband. The experience of childbirth, her physical punishment of her son, and the connection, at the end of the novel, with her deceased mother, mark a cultural and personal recuperation for Marie.

Although Joey appears to be at ease with his body, whether it is during physical activity, such as hockey and work, or in his sexual interaction with women, he is at a loss when he tries to understand his social context and the nature of his relations with others. This sense of inadequacy is partly due to his sheltered and structured life as a member of the Barone household. The death of his father, which upturns the order of things, is profoundly upsetting for him. Forced to rethink the assumptions underlying his existence, Joey concedes that his distrust of words and the act of communication has severed him emotionally from his parents:

> He felt himself choking with the need to tell [Assunta] how much she meant to him. How much he had hidden his love for her and Adamo in a stupid reticence that couldn't be excused by any differences in language or culture. (170)

The binary of mind and body, which is attached to specific social values and supported by seemingly opposed models of behaviour, continually folds into itself because the individual character is caught in a complex array of social and personal tendencies. In the words of Linda Hutcheon, who paraphrases George Lipsitz,

since ethnic and racial minorities can neither assimilate
nor separate completely from the dominant culture, they
are forced into 'complex and creative cultural negotiations' with and against the dominant force, negotiations
that involve confronting it with its own history and traditions.

Splitting, 52

Marie's and Joey's narratives, then, are mirrors of
each other, reflecting images of the same cultural
problematic with the shared hope of resolution.

6. *Unclosed Narration*

Closure is problematized by the uncertainty of the
conclusion whose thematic frame, imagery, and symbolism overflow with conflicting meanings. In the
penultimate segment of the novel, the merging of
Marie and Joey's narratives is supported by the circular movement of both narratives back to the Barone
home: from Adamo's wake to Assunta's funeral and
the subsequent reuniting of brother and sister. This
circularity appears to signal the reunification of the
protagonists' ethnicity, and is undermined by the
ambiguity of the end.

Marie and Joey show their love for each other
through an emotional farewell at the airport, but their
lives are still proceeding in different directions. Marie
is returning to her roots, displayed in her flight to the
old country, and Joey is departing from Little Italy,
the community that protected his parents from the
assimilative pressures of the new world and kept them

grounded in their cultural traditions. Even though
Marie and Joey have come to terms with their Italian
ancestry, their identities remain inconclusive and mu-
table. Preparing to attend her cousin's wedding in
Assunta's hometown, Marie temporarily leaves behind a troubled marriage, knowing that its survival is
far from certain. Although she has re-embraced the
old neighbourhood, the demolition of the refurbished
houses is clearing space for a new commercial enterprise, the building of the International Bridge. Social
and economic factors are forever refashioning the
culture of the first generation. This image of flux is
supplemented by the sale of the family home. The trip
to Italy suggests that Marie is moving towards some
new and undefined way of being since she cannot
resume her life in the Italian community or continue
to live uncritically in mainstream society.

This ambivalence is consolidated through the
overarching image of the brick pyramid at the end of
the novel. Joey constructs a huge brick pyramid in the
back garden of his parents' house from which "he
derive[s] immense satisfaction" (198). The protagonist's reconciliation with his immigrant culture is
exhibited in the way he prepares the bricks: "Joey
buttered the brick slowly" (197) – which simulates
the domestic activity of his mother, and by the fact
that he uses his father's "tools" (198) and celebrates
his craftsmanship. The brick pyramid appears to be
an expression of Joey's acceptance of the immigrant
heritage.

The picture of the pyramid in the backyard encapsulates aspects of immigrant life in Canada. The artisanship of the old world, such as bricklaying, which is represented by the construction of the pyramid, is employed by the immigrant in order to survive economically in the new country. The pyramid is built next to the vegetable garden in the backyard, which is a remnant of the immigrant's agrarian past. There is an ironic undertone to the brick pyramid: the pyramid hints at both redemption and loss. In erecting the monument, Joey commemorates his parents' achievements in the Sault and elegizes the traditional culture. This incongruity is supported by the contradiction that although the pyramid is almost invincible ". . . would be hard to tear down" (198) – it is ultimately a temporary structure: "he was making something that wouldn't last" (198). As a manifestation of Joey's state of mind, the pyramid personifies opposed ideas about the endurance and precariousness of Italian Canadian identity.

Annalise's ironic statement pinpoints the pyramid's equivocality:

> "It's elemental," she said, grinning at him. "It has inertia. And it's ambiguous." (197)

The many meanings of the pyramid reside in the contradiction that while its size implies vitality, its mass betrays a type of stasis. This irony recurs in the final image of the novel, in which fragmentation and resolution go hand in hand: "Then he split the last brick in half and placed it on the very top" (198). The

irony does not end here, for the pyramid is juxtaposed
to the steel plant, which is emblematic of the dominance of industrialization over the small Italian enclave. This juxtaposition spawns a variety of
antithetical meanings about the interface between
agrarian and urban society.

The pyramid will be torn down by a wrecker's ball
as capitalist enterprise flattens the reconstituted village of Little Italy. Nevertheless, industrial society has
provided Italian immigrants with economic opportunities which, in turn, allowed them to build their
community. The planned leveling of the old neighbourhood, while it pushes Joey out of the family
home, is synchronic with his decision to leave the
enclave and live with his girlfriend, Annalise. Joey's
departure supports the attitude of other second generation Italians who want to be on their own or are
about to purchase expensive homes in the suburbs.
The protagonist's evolution is characterized by movement and contradiction, for the moment of destruction also signals the possibility of change.

Through the image of the brick pyramid, *Black
Madonna* encapsulates its unique reading of Italian
Canadian identity. The brick pyramid epitomizes
ideas about ancestral lineage, about the importance
of cultural and familial continuity. At the same time,
the impending annihilation of the structure symbolizes the transitoriness of Italian immigrant culture,
encompassing the passage of the first generation and
the modification of the identities of the second generation. The building of the pyramid is, figuratively

speaking, about the making, unmaking, and remaking of the subjectivity of the ethnic protagonist, in which the past is merged with the present in an ongoing process of transformation. The representation of "Italianness" as complex and discontinuous, and as constantly being reshaped by given social forces, does not erase the distinct identities of the Italian-descended characters. The cultural "particularity" of the protagonists and the "Italianness" of the subject matter remain the central foci of *Black Madonna* (Waxman, 22) Such a multifarious depiction of ethnicity is especially manifest in Minni's *Other Selves* and Ricci's *Lives of the Saints*. These two literary texts examine the problems with and the contradictions and ambiguities of Italian peasant culture only to assert its importance in the identity formation of the ethnic protagonist. It is this kind of attachment to cultural roots which strongly underlies the development of narrative in *Black Madonna*.

WORKS CITED

Beddoes, Julie. "Sandor, Alex and the rest: multiplication of the subject in John Marlyn's *Under the Ribs of Death*," *Open Letter* 6, 8 (1985).

Hutcheon, Linda. *Splitting Images: Contemporary Canadian Ironies.* Toronto: U. of T. Press, 1991.

_____. "'A Lightness of thoughtfulness': The Power of Postmodern Irony," *Open Letter* 8, 1 (1991).

Mandel, Eli. "Introduction," *Under the Ribs of Death* by John Marlyn. Toronto: McClelland and Stewart, 1971.

Paci, F.G. *Black Madonna.* Ottawa: Oberon Press, 1982.

_____. "Tasks of the Canadian Novelist Writing on Immigrant Themes," *Contrasts: Comparative Essays on Italian-Canadian*

Writing. ed. J. Pivato. Montreal: Guernica Editions, 1985.

Sciff-Zamaro, Roberta. "*Black Madonna:* A Search for the Great Mother," in *Contrasts.*

Waxman, Martin. "Profile, Frank Paci: The Discipline of Discovery," *Books in Canada* (Nov. 1994).

FATHER AND FAMILY

The "Padre Pardone" figure in Frank Paci's The Italians *and Antonio Casella's* The Sensualist

GAETANO RANDO

Italian-Canadian literature presents both interesting parallels and differences with respect to its Italian-Australian counterpart. Although there has been an Italian presence in both Australia for almost 200 years, in Canada for over 300 years, and some writings by Italian immigrants appeared in the nineteenth century and the first half of the twentieth century, it is essentially a phenomenon of the last half century and coincides both with post-war Italian mass immigration to Canada and Australia and with the rise of the Trudeauian concept of multiculturalism also adopted by Australia. The themes in Italian Canadian narrative seem to parallel those of Italian-Australian narrative – exile, alienation, emargination, the concept of community, family values, generational conflicts, the question if not the resolution of identity, the relationship with the old country and the new one, traditional verses new culture – although the emphasis and treatment given to these themes are often different. There are also other differences. Ital-

ian-Canadian writers as a group, though not necessarily on an individual basis, write in four languages:
dialect,[1] "standard" Italian, English and French with
some works being rewritten or translated from one
language to the other, whereas the Italian-Australian
group of writers uses dialect, "standard" Italian and
English with rewriting or translation from one language to the other occurring rarely. Another notable
difference is the presence of sizable group of 1B[2] and
second generation Italian-Canadian writers, university educated, socially mobile and articulate who not
only write in English and/or French but also make the
effort to write in Italian, an element which is so far
largely lacking among Italian Australian 1B and second generation writers. It is largely the work of these
writers, in a Canadian cultural context which accepts
difference more readily than the Australian one, that
has led to the opening up of a more substantial critical
debate than in the Australian case.

Against the background of these similarities and
differences a comparison between Italian Canadian
and Italian Australian writing should offer some interesting perspectives on the Italian diaspora experience which could include, among other things:

- The function and role of the writer and their relationship to the respective host societies;

- Discussion of the sociological nature of these texts (realist
  elements) and their role in providing an articulation on
  behalf of those who could not speak of the hardships,
  struggles and price of the migrant experience;

- Their status as a "minority literature within a minority literature" (Pivato 1985a:11);

- Their contribution to the debate on host society (Canadian or Australian respectively) cultural identity.

An exhaustive treatment of these issues would clearly require a much more lengthy and ambitious study than the present one which, nonetheless, proposes a starting point through the comparative examination of perceptions of *padre* and *famiglia* presented in two novels, *The Italians* by Italian Canadian writer Frank Paci (Paci 1978) and *The Sensualist* by Italian Australian writer Antonio Casella (Casella 1991). The two novels share a realist interpretation, contain some interesting parallels in narrative technique as well as the centrality of themes relating to these concepts with both differences and similarities in treatment and detail due in part to their different settings and the different life experiences of their authors. Sciff-Zamaro's (1985:80) comment that Paci in his novels "has turned to the old family myths and beliefs of the Mediterranean" can to a large extent also be applied to Casella.

Antonio Casella migrated to Western Australia with his family from a small mountain village in Sicily in 1959 at the age of fifteen, with no knowledge of English. During his first years in Australia he worked in an iron foundry, as a painter, and briefly at the Wittenoom asbestos mine while attending night classes. At the age of twenty-five he enrolled at Uni-

versity and in 1974 became a secondary school
teacher. As well as *The Sensualist* he has published
Southfalia, an allegorical satire (Casella 1980), a fantasy novel based on the concept of Western Australia
as a colony established by the ancient Romans. Despite having migrated at age fifteen, Casella as a writer
is comparable to 1B generation Italian Australian
novelists in that he has published exclusively in English.

Casella's The *Senualist* relates the story of the
Amedeo family narrated by Joyce and Nick Amedeo,
by Nick's employee Steve Lambert and (but only the
final chapter) by Nick's daughter Nella. From his
beginnings as a poorly educated child migrant who
arrived in Fremantle in 1938 and commenced working as an unskilled labourer, Nick Amedeo has
achieved substantial material success in the construction business during his forty or so years in Australia
developing considerable technical and entrepreneurial
skills in the process. Nick is not superstitious and does
not subscribe to the traditional Italian peasant belief
in *malocchio* but knowing about it makes him wary
of people's envy of his success in business and with
women (Casella 1991:82). The secret of his success
lies in his ability to change and be changed. He has a
mansion, a Mercedes, a retinue of dependents, a
devoted Australian wife and a Greek Australian mis-
tress. However, events conspire to upset the cosy
solid world he has created and a succession of devel-
opments forces both Joyce and Nick to confront
themselves and their personal histories as well as the

relationship each has with their two children, their son John who rejects Nick's success and the prospect of joining his father's business and their daughter Nella who is vibrantly positive towards her parents but insists on following her own path in life. The past invades the present as they embark on separate journeys into the world of their early childhood and adolescence. Joyce's journey through dream and memory takes her to the north-west of Western Australia, a vast alien world feared by its white inhabitants, while Nick returns in spirit to the myths and rituals of the harsh environment of the mountains of Sicily.

Frank Paci emigrated to Canada from Pesaro with his parents in 1952 at the age of four years and grew up in Sault Ste. Marie, Ontario. His first novel *The Italians* was followed by seven other novels with a ninth, *Italian Shoes,* which deals with the return journey to Italy by the 1B generation central character. *The Italians* became a bestseller and has also been published in a French translation (1990) but it is his second novel *Black Madonna* (1982) that has so far proved to be his most popular book.

Paci's *The Italians* narrates the story of the Gaetano family from the standpoint of Lorianna the daughter, Alberto the father, Bill the youngest son and Aldo the eldest son with Giulia the mother having no part in the narration although she is distinctly present as a character. Some twenty years after migrating from Romagna to the steel-producing town of Marionville in northern Canada, Alberto has achieved some of the goals that led him to leave the old country. At the cost of forsaking his talents as a musician and an *artigiano,* he has become a leading hand and valued worker at the local steel plant, the *miseria* he and Giulia had experienced in the old country is a thing of the past though still a shadow on the present despite their well-stocked cellar and they are proud owners of the house painstakingly renovated and refurbished by Alberto. Their children are nicely on the way to being *sistemati* (Lorianna through marriage and the two sons in contexts that promise to take them away from a working-class future), despite some worrying interferences and considerable generational friction in the process. All this, however, changes when Alberto has a life-threatening accident at the plant bringing each member of the family to confront both their essential self and their relationships with each other.

The concepts of *padre* and *famiglia* can thus be seen as central themes in both novels and in this sense both present a family saga although in Paci's case the theme of family saga is found in other novels such as *The Father* (1984) while the *Black Blood* series of five novels depicting the growth of practical, cultural and literary wisdom of the central character Marco Trecroci with its associated distancing from his ethnic roots in the initial stages and eventual reconciliation (Paci 1991-2002) is clearly a more deeply expressed family saga of greater proportions.

In both *The Italians* and *The Sensualist* the father (Alberto and Nick) is the founder/initiator of the principle of the importance of the family, and it is interesting how in Casella this is seen as a highly positive personal value by the Australian "outsider" Steve Lambert (son of a weak and alcohol-ridden father) who considers Nick Amedeo not only an employed but a father figure he never had: "working for Nick isn't just a job for me, it's a lifestyle. I enjoy the fishing trips, the sessions at the club, the family do's. In a sense Nick's family is my family" (Casella 1991:19).

Both Alberto and Nick see the family as the most fundamental social unit, worthy of hard work and sacrifices and a tower of strength against the social and economic insecurity often endemic in the history of their respective regions. Both fathers also have a dynastic concept of family and see their continuity in their children as a form of immortality. For Alberto the family is the justification for migration, for day-to-day toil and for the sacrifices that characterise his life in Canada. It is also seen as the basis for continuity of traditional "Italian" values in the new country, a continuity partially achieved in *The Italians* with the eldest son espousing the priesthood and the daughter and younger son marrying and producing children as well as a dynamic continuation of the family in stages of transition from Italian first generation to Italian Canadian second generation and potentially to Canadian third generation. In *The Sensualist* Nick perceives the family as part of the empire he has created whose purpose is to "carry on your blood" (Casella 1991:141) and wants his family to be seen as perfect by outsiders (Casella 1991:55-56) although internally it presents dysfunctional elements (Joyce's anxiety, John's rebelliousness and self-hatred, Nella's insistence on doing her own thing). He is in a sense attempting to recreate his own original Sicilian family with himself in a role analogous to that assumed by his patriarchal *nonno*. But his dynastic ambitions for family continuity and for the family business (Amedeo & Son, Casella 1991:59) he has painstakingly created are thwarted by his son's refusal and subsequent dissipation of most of the wealth created by his father. Family breakdown and dissipation of the business after Nick's death and Joyce's subsequent stroke seems to mark the end of Nick's power and ambition. However the marriage of the daughter and the birth of Nick's "Australian" grandchildren at the end of the novel provides continuity in a phoenix-like resurrection through a blending of Italian and Australian family values, a note of regeneration and hope similar to that observable for Paci's *Black Madonna*.

The two novels present interesting variations on Pivato's (1994:175, 177) observation that the depiction of fragmentation in the Italian migrant family contradicts the popular myth of close family unity and support. In Casella there is considerable internal fragmentation in an apparently "united" Amedeo family with varying degrees of estrangement between the individual members while the Gaetano family in Paci's novel moves through a phase of fragmentation and, again, varying degrees of estrangement to a newly constituted unity under parameters that are different to those operating in traditional Italian peasant culture.

The father figure is central to the concept of *famiglia* in both novels although the larger than life and somewhat flamboyant Nick seems more domineering and controlling and to some extent less preoccupied with family in *The Sensualist* than Alberto, with his constant attempts to monitor, guide and worry about his children's lives according to his own beliefs, in *The Italians*. Both seem to claim a patriarchal if not maschilist position within the family unit with their wives being relegated to background roles (Giulia more so than Joyce) and both preside over some aspects of traditional practices. Alberto attempts to recreate the old world within a limited environment by the ritual acceptance of his duty to his family, the games of *briscola* with family and friends, making his own wine, playing his accordion when his *compare* visits (with nostalgic memories of pre-war *feste paesane* in the old country), building a basement that "provided an atmosphere like the stucco dwellings that . . . were native to the old country" (Paci 1978:46) and stocking it with wine and traditional foods (Paci 1978:113). By comparison Nick's links with traditional cultural practices are closely related to his relationship with his grandfather and he seems less concerned with a surface recreation of aspects of the old world although his expectation that his wife be virtuous (Casella 1991:52) is clearly linked to Sicilian traditions of *onestà* and *onore* for the woman while his sexual adventures are in keeping with traditional Sicilian concepts of masculinity. Nick believes the old folk were right about marriage and children being permanent (Casella 1991:84), a view that is in direct contract with that of his Anglo-Australian bank manager Hugh O'Donnell who has been through three marriages and has an indeterminate number of kids to support.

Nick's cellar (an unusual feature in an Australian house) with its stores of wine and traditional foods not necessarily there to be eaten (Casella 1991:194-5) is strikingly similar to Alberto's but assumes an additional dimension as confirmation of his dominance and power through its function as his private inner sanctum where the transformation of the pig (a great luxury during Nick's childhood in Sicily) takes place. In this ritual, carried out with quasi-religious observance, Nick emulates his grandfather's role as *padre padrone* in the preparation and distribution of the Christmas *capretto*. However, he is unable to emulate some of his role model's characteristics (cannot command absolute obedience and respect from his children) and it is only after considerable searching both in memory and in conversations with his uncle Basili that Nick becomes aware of a hither unknown aspect of his grandfather's character (his observance of the honour code resulting in the slaying of Nick's mother, a traumatic experience that Nick witnesses and suppresses until the present time).

An interesting counterpoint to the figures of the two fathers is provided through the characters Lorenzo, Alberto's son in law and Steve, Nick's employee cum protégé. At the beginning of the *The Italians* Lorenzo, whose Calabrian origins are under-scored, is cast in the role of the archetypal domineer-ing Southern Italian husband who wants everything his own way ("A wife, she goes to church; a husband goes to work," Paci 1978:53) and expects his wife to be subservient both sexually and domestically. He forces sex on Lorianna, does not consider it his role to help with household chores, makes all the decisions (a new car rather than a more comfortable home), refuses to fit in to the new country and is respectful towards his father in law though refusing any inter-ference in his family or work-related affairs. How-ever, as the novel progresses Lorenzo's promotion at the steel plant, Lorianna's empowerment as the mother of his children and Alberto's accident all combine to make the marriage a sharing relationship with Lorianna no longer in a subservient role but on an equal footing and Lorenzo willing to accept some aspects of the new country. Steve Lambert looks to Nick as a role model in much the same way as Nick looked to his grandfather, giving him the respect and obedience that grandfather received from his sons and that, paradoxically, Nick does not receive from his own son John. Steve not only follows through on Nick's directions and decisions at work even against his own better judgment but he is also Nick's constant companion in after-work activities, thus filling the void left by John's rejection, which range from help-ing him choose a present for Joyce's birthday to accompanying him on fishing trips and assisting him

in the preparation of the pig. Steve's admiration for
Nick and the recognition for his charisma is almost
total, the only exception being that Steve does not
treat women (Lily) in the same way Nick treats
women. It is perhaps no coincidence that after Nick's
death Steve ends up connected to Nick's family
through Nella's marriage to his brother and that his
sense of family loyalty makes him instrumental in
ensuing an ongoing relationship between his child
and Nick's grandchildren despite the different socio-
economic status of the two families. However, he
changes from a nice, quiet and chubby man to one
who is obsessed with diet and fitness because his
marriage to Lily has led to the formation of a dysfunctional family and the frenetic chase after money
(329).[3]

Another counterpoint to the father/husband figure is presented by the wives in the two novels.
Giulia's role in *The Italians* is determined by the
traditional peasant view of the husband/wife relationship (a role also partially accepted but to a large extent
rejected by Lorianna in her marriage to the first
generation Calabrian Lorenzo) where the wife's basic
function is to care for the family and act as a custodian
of traditional cultural values. Her situation depicted
in the novel closely correlates to sociological obser-
vations on the role of Italian migrant women as
cultural custodians and cultural brokers often inaccu-
rately portrayed as oppressive/oppressed, helpless
and illiterate peasant types (Vasta 1992:153-154). A
largely passive participant, at least on a surface level,

Giulia expresses herself through cooking (Paci 1978:74-75). Her life is lived completely inside her children (Paci 1978:78) and to some extent parallels Assunta Barone in *Black Madonna* (Paci 1982). Her emigration to Canada was not voluntarily but imposed by her husband (another correlation with sociological observation – Rando, 1992:188-189) and, compared to Alberto's ambivalent attitudes, she displays nostalgia for the old country blaming Alberto for having uprooted them whenever the family suffers a setback (Paci 1978:156). The silence that envelops Giulia Gaetano and Assunta Barone is paralleled in a minor character in Casella's novel, a Calabrian widow who bursts into speech when she discovers Nick understands dialect because "her own children speak to her in English, even the little ones, she has become a foreigner in her own home" (Casella 1991:184).[4] Joyce's role, on the other hand, is a more prominent and interactive one and certainly not cast in a traditional Italian mold despite an apparent dependency on and a passive resistance to Nick's overwhelming presence. Joyce is in the grips of a personal/existentialist dilemma and suffers acute depression (Casella 1991:64-65) arising from a sense of uncertainty, lack of confidence and fear of having inherited her mother's paranoia. She is of an "old" anglo-celtic Australian pioneer family and attempts to find a sense of identity through her union with Nick, a "new" NESB Australian. In fact, their ethnic and sociocultural backgrounds are vastly different despite some similarities in the landscapes associated with their

formative years (both Sicily and rural Western Australia are harsh arid lands that inspire isolation, strong
feelings, and a sense of mystery).[5] Her relationship
with Nick is not only based on strong sexual attrac-
tion, their children and the sharing of worldly goods
but also has a spiritual element. Nick's energy and
highly positive attitude to life contrasts with and
complements Joyce's greater perspicacity but less
positive attitude, self-doubts and uncertainty about
her sanity. Although she loves him and accepts some
of his traditional practices, including his infidelities,
she is considering leaving him partly because of the
fear that she might have inherited her mother's paranoia, partly because of the desire to claim her own
space. Ultimately, however, her life experience with
Nick leads to the final realisation that she is, after all,
a vital link in the chain of destiny and has been
instrumental in helping to shape a new world (Casella
1991:334), a realisation that puts her on an equal
footing with Nick and leads her to the achievement
of union with him in the hereafter.

The children in the two families display different
ways of resolving (or not resolving) the ambivalence
of operating within the Italian and Canadian/Austra-
lian cultures, of coming to terms (or not) with their
bi-cultural ethnic identity and of negotiating their
relationship with their parents. Alberto's children
partially reconcile their inner conflicts after an act of
sacrifice in the interests of family solidarity (Minni
1985:8) whereas of Nick's children it is only Nella
who finds self-realization through the reconstitution

of the family while John continues on the path of self-destruction caused by the rejection of family bonds.

For Italian born Aldo the priesthood is initially seen as an escape from a Canadian context in which he feels a misfit (Paci 1978:61) but the sacrifice he makes for his father when he is on the verge of renouncing his calling ("if his father lived he would take his deacon's vows without any further ado . . . He was Italian and had to pay the price," Paci 1978:144) is both a reconciliation with his past and an acceptance of his responsibilities with the suggestion that there is the potential for adaptation to the new environment. Lorianna, also Italian born, chooses to marry Lorenzo rather that embrace a religious calling perhaps because of parental expectations which include some subtle maneuvering in convincing her to accept Lorenzo for fear that she might marry a non Italian (Paci 1987:61). Initially she does not know if she is Italian or Canadian which leads her to stray from her parent's world in a complex confusion of mixed loyalties, sense of belonging and feelings of guilt. However, as the novel progresses tradition seems to "kick in" (though only after Lorenzo has modified his traditional Italian attitudes) bringing her to the realization "that she was neither Canadian nor Italian, but simply a member of a family which was part of something larger" (Paci 1978:133). Another significant element in the resolution of Lorianna's dilemma is her view of Angelina as her covenant with the new country (Paci 1978:51)[6] and her role cultural broker for both her husband and her parents. Canadian born Bill is the sibling who displays the most overt rejection of his Italian roots. His ambition of becoming a professional ice-hockey star player (despite his father seeing ice-hockey as deviant) is his way of identifying with Canada and of becoming accepted into the new society. However, his father's accident brings him to the realisation of his ties with his parents and his responsibilities to them. The banquet given by the Italian community in his honour makes him aware of a strong bond between himself and the community and the pride he feels for these migrants with "work-weary faces" (Paci 1978:197) for whom he has become a symbol of a sense of belonging in the new country.

John's aversion to his father, beginning at an early age and intensifying as he grows up, is blamed on the faulty Hathaway genes (Casella 1991:59, 61). There is also a suggestion that mixed parentage could be a factor and that John may have inherited some of the negative traits of *nonno*'s illegitimate son Saru who was very much the black sheep of the family. John stands in stark contrast with Steve Lambert (Casella 1991:61) who is the son/friend to Nick that John is not and is accepted into the Amedeo family (but not to the point that Nick thinks of offering him partnership in the firm). Nick sometimes thinks of Steve as his would-be usurper and John as his would-be heir (Casella 1991:83), wants to dominate them both and be in control. John is arrogant, unruly to the point of sometimes engaging in brawls, a snob (he regards

Steve as a hired hand), sullen, has a somewhat morbid attachment to his mother, considers that everything is owed to him and is successful with women (his only attribute which pleases Nick). Although an accountant by profession, his real activity seems to be partying and drinking in an attempt to blot out an eternally unresolved existentialist anguish. In drinking he displays a characteristic commonly attributed by Italian Australian narrative writers to their Anglo-Australian characters (see, for example, Cappiello 1981 and Nibbi 1965) while his destructive behaviour can be seen indicative of the self-hatred that is a common condition of people of minority groups in the Canadian cultural context (Pivato 1994:207).[7] The relationship between John and Nick presents considerable contrast to Nick's relationship with his daughter Nella (Casella 1991:60) who is vibrant, full of life, and displays Amedeo zest, pride and spirit of independence, elements that together add up to a positive sense of identity. Initially Nella seems very "Australian." She does not want to get married, seeing it as a loss of freedom, but eventually does after her father's death and the subsequent loss, through John's disastrous actions, of the fortune Nick had painstakingly built up. Her marriage to Geoff Lambert (Steve's brother) a charismatic Christian idealist with little sense of practicality leads Nella to take on the role of the practical one in the family (the youngest of the two boys, Michael, is impulsive, wimpish, aggressive and resembles his grandfather). Nella displays the best of both parental legacies: Sicilian resilience and survival, instinctive love and passion; Australian tolerance, moral strength and rationality (Casella 1991:322).

To some extent relationships within the migrant family are influenced by the different perspectives that each member has on environment, culture, identity and language and the need to accommodate often contradictory positions within the same family unit (Loh 1980:134-135). Both novels present some of these aspects in varying degrees.

For the Italian born family members the relationship with the old country presents metaphysical values somehow superior to the value system of the new country although some aspects of the relationship are unresolved and possibly unresolvable. The migration experience of Alberto, Giulia and, to a lesser extent, Nick represents substantial uprooting from their peasant origins although it is a release from *miseria* for Alberto (despite a life somehow happier than in Canada) and a distancing from a traumatic childhood experience as well as the eventual acquisition of wealth for Nick (despite his sense of belonging to his grandfather's family). For Lorianna the migration process results in a lost childhood and, as she grows older, the feeling that the old country seems to be calling her back with greater force, the release from the grudge she had against her parents (Paci 1978:72) and the not entirely unambiguous possibility of taking her daughter, Angelina, back for a visit (Paci 1978:71). Alberto too has ambivalent attitudes about visiting the old country (and then only if he can return as a "victorious Canadian," Paci 1978:129, an attitude also enunciated in the Italian Australian context in Cappiello 1981:84) despite nostalgia and his limited existence in the new country while Joyce suspects that Nick does not want to go back but does not know the reason why (Casella 1991:62). At a surface level Nick does not display a feeling of loss for the old country and seems to have totally accepted Australian value systems to the extent that even as a young man he "spoke Australian like one of the [Wonga] locals, much to everyone's amazement" (Casella 1991:23). As a consequence his children do not have any connections with or feelings for Italy. His re-evocation of childhood memories in the days preceding his death is entirely internalised and seems to be a quest for self-knowledge as well as an attempt to reach an understanding of the tragedy that struck his parents although some aspects of the event (*nonno*'s role in the honour killing, whether Saru is Nick's real father) can never be resolved with absolute certainty.

Joyce has never visited Sicily and her view of the island is in part embodied in Nick's vitality and sensuality although her perceptions of its social and geographical characteristics are mediated not so much by Nick but by her uncle Desmond and sister Flo. Young Joyce at Binji Cross is fascinated by Desmond's tales of the classical Mediterranean world including the idyllic view of Sicily as a "country of eagle's nest villages hanging precariously from white clay ridges in the sun . . . the island of shepherds that knew acardian joys and smelled of civilisations." (Casella 1991:4). Flo, who has visited Nick's home

village, finds it "dirty and unkempt" (Casella
1991:87), its inhabitants like the Aborigines (in fact,
Flo cannot understand where Nick got his boundless
energy) although the countryside is quite inspiring
"with more arrogance than a beauty queen" and
white stone ridges as lonely as the Australian outback
(Casella 1991:88) thus providing a point of contact
with Joyce's own origins for Joyce too is a migrant to
urban Perth from "a land where a woman, more so
than a man, might be lost and none would notice. A
country that still mourned its sparse down of she-oaks
and salmon gums; a landscape that listened for the
music of black-boys played like zithers by the easter-
lies" (Casella 1991:4).

Perceptions of the new country are somewhat
different in the two novels. Nick's sense of identification with Australia is highly positive and enthusiastic
("This is the country, this is the life!" Casella
1991:79) since it has allowed him to achieve not only
considerable material success but also a sense of great
personal achievement ("it doesn't matter who your
father was, it's what you do that counts." Casella
1991:28) both in business and in family life. He is
proud of the contribution made by Italians to the
transformation of Australia ("When we got there all
you could see was asbestos and weatherboard shacks
. . . In the fifties we started building in bricks and made
money by the bucketfull," Casella 1991:102). Alberto's sense of identification with Canada is much
more qualified. While appreciating the material bene-
fits of life in the new country and how they have been

instrumental in allowing him to provide for his family, he is also aware that this has been achieved at the cost of a less rich and varied life and of daily toil both through his work at the steel plant (economically viable because of the migrant workforce) as well as the time and effort required to repair and refurbish his home. For Alberto Canadian values are questionable, in some cases incomprehensible, and present the potential "loss" of his children. He considers ice hockey deviant and cannot understand Bill's passion for the sport nor why he leaves school to play the game professionally.[8] Aldo's religious crisis, which dashes the high expectations he had for his son, is, in Alberto's view, triggered by Aldo's relationship with the Canadian Evylyn while Lorianna's less than ideal marriage to Lorenzo is welcomed because he is not Canadian. In fact, Lorenzo's initial position in refusing to accept any of the ways of the new country (including the language) is instrumental in provoking Lorianna's desperate marital plight. It is only through his gradual acceptance of the new country (including the language) and the imminent birth of the second child that he sees Lorianna as an equal partner and his new family as meaningful.

Although the two novels deal with the migration experience and indeed present certain aspects of the universality of that experience, they are vastly different in detail, context, focus and resolution. Despite these differences Casella too seems to adhere to the conceptualisation expressed by Paci that "In this world we live on a bumpy road of surface reality and abstract reality . . . Reality in the novel . . . includes all differences – all parts – because it sees that only the whole is truth." (Paci 1985:39,40).

The Italians presents a family most of whose members came from the gentle countryside of central Italy to settle in an industrial Canadian town characterised by cold and ice as well as the presence of an Italian community. *The Sensualist* deals with an individual who migrates from the harsh Sicilian countryside to an Australian city characterised by heat and dust, founding there a family and a fortune, but does not deal with the Italian community present in that city in real life. Spiritual values seem to dominate in the Gaetano family (Paci 1994:203) despite the apparent lack of such values in the new country whereas they are not present in the Amedeo family and it is in fact Nella who manages to sidetrack Steve's brother Geoff from his religious calling as a charismatic Christian by seducing and subsequently marrying him. Nick's desire to dominate and not to "give ground" indirectly causes his death, an event which leads his daughter to reconciliation with her heritage but which irrevocably loses his son. Alberto's more modest character draws family together after his accident with his children in their turn making sacrifices to help their parents and Alberto "stepping down" from his role of *paterfamilias*. As in *Black Madonna* (see Pivato 1994:188) *The Italians* ends on a note of regeneration and hope both for the original Gaetano family and the new families (Lorianna's and Bill's) that are being formed.

In the final analysis, however, both novels are about the passing of the *padre padrone* figure, the transition from traditional old country family values to something which is a blend of both the old and the new with the daughters "taking charge" as both cultural custodians and cultural innovators and producing children who resemble their grandfathers. The family remains the focal unit, a source of unity and strength for all its members, but is redefined a new tradition, respectively Italian Australian and Italian Canadian with new roles and new relationships for the people who comprise it.

NOTES

1   Exclusively in poetry, e.g. Corrado Mastropasqua, *'Na lacrema e 'na risa*, Napoli, 1969.

2   Generally referred to persons who are born in the country of origin of the parents (in this case Italy) but who migrate to the new country at a relatively early age and received all or nearly all their education there.

3   This characteristic of NESB (non-English speaking background) migrant families finds further elaboration in Cappiello (1981: 19-20, 33, 43, 70) who considers the adoption of crass materialistic values a highly negative influence of the host society.

4   In Paci there are no "silent" male characters whereas another minor character in *The Sensualist*, Pino, the silent contemplative pessimistic creative jewel-maker who wanted to go to university in Italy, has lost the ability to explain in Italian but has not gained the ability to explain in English (Casella 1991: 243). Another male character in Gabbrielli's (2000) novel, the retired Sicilian miner Angelo who lives in a small Western Australian aboriginal settlement, finds great difficulty in expressing himself in Italian after 70 years in Australia.

5   The arid harshness and the sense of mystery presented by the

Australian outback is a theme found in a number of Italian Australian writers. Particularly interesting examples are Leoni (1982) and Gabbrielli (1988, 2000).

6   The concept of a covenant through the children born in the new country is also found in Di Stefano (1996).

7   Self-hatred is less apparent in Australian migrant literature although in can be found as a central theme in a few works. For example, in "La giornataccia di Montefiore" (Andreoni, 1978) the central character Philip Montefiore, a second generation Italian Australian who completely suppresses his Italian roots in a attempt to gain the acceptance of the conservative rural NSW Australian community where he is posted as manager of the local bank, becomes violently ill when he attempts to "blend in" by emulating local beer-drinking habits.

8   Sports as a new country identifier expressed through ice hockey is an important theme in some of Paci's novels. It is virtually non existent in Italian Australian narrative despite the considerable value placed on sport in Australia. The only short story that presents sports as a central theme is Fusillo's (1987) *Memories of Sunday cricket in the Street*, while the protagonist of Andreoni's (1982) *Cenere* becomes captain of the First XI at school as part of an all-out effort to become completely Australian.

WORKS CITED

Andreoni, Giovanni (1982) *Cenere* in Andreoni, *L'italo-australiano come linguaggio letterario. Un racconto documentario.* Rome: Il Veltro Editrice.

_____ (1978). "La giornataccia di Montefiore" in Andreoni, *La lingua degli Italani d'Australia e altri racconti.* Roma: Il Veltro Editrice.

Cappiello, Rosa (1981). *Paese fortunato.* Milano: Feltrinelli.

Casella, Antonio (1980). *Southfalia, an allegorical satire.* Fremantle, W.A.: Fremantle Arts Centre Press.

_____ (1991). *The Sensualist.* Rydalmere, NSW: Hodder & Stoughton.

Di Stefano, Enoe (1996). *L'avventura australiana: vivere il mondo con fede tenace.* Camposampiero, PD: Edizioni del noce.

Fusillo, Archimede (1987). *Memories of Sunday cricket in the Street*. Melbourne: Macmillan.

Gabbrielli, Emilio (2000). *Polenta e Goanna*. Florence: Pontecorboli.

Leoni, Franko (1983). "La memorabile biografia di Carlo di Priamo, vignaio da Poggibonsi," in Gaetano Rando, ed. *Italian Writers in Australia: Essays and Texts*. Wollongong, NSW: University of Wollongong, Department of Modern Languages.

Loh, Morag (1980). *With Courage in their Cases*. Melbourne: FILEF.

Minni, C.D. (1985). "An Interview with Frank Paci," *Canadian Literature*, 106: 5-15.

Nibbi, Gino (1965). *Cocktails d'Australia*. Milano: Martello.

Paci, F.G. (1978). *The Italians*. Ottawa: Oberon Press.

_____ (1982). *Black Madonna*. Ottawa: Oberon Press.

_____ (1984). *The Father*. Ottawa: Oberon Press.

_____ (1985). "Tasks of the Canadian Novelist Writing on Immigrant Themes," in Pivato, 1985: 35-60.

_____(1990). *La Famille Gaetano*. Trans. of *The Italians* by Robert Paquin. Montreal: Guernica.

_____ (1991). *Black Blood*. Ottawa: Oberon Press.

_____(1992). *Under the Bridge*. Ottawa: Oberon Press.

_____ (2002). *Italian Shoes*. Toronto: Guernica Editions.

Pivato, Joseph. ed. (1985). *Contrasts: Comparative Essays on Italian-Canadian Writing*. Montreal: Guernica Editions.

_____ (1994). *Echo: Essays on Other Literatures*. Toronto: Guernica Editions.

Rando, Gaetano (1992). "Narrating the migration experience," in Stephen Castles, Caroline Alcorso, Gaetano Rando & Ellie Vasta, eds. *Australia's Italians: Culture and Community in a Changing Society*. Sydney: Allen & Unwin, 184-201.

Sciff-Zamaro, Roberta (1985). "*Black Madonna*: A Search for the Great Mother,"in Pivato, 1985: 77-99.

Vasta, Ellie (1992). "Italian migrant women" in Stephen Castles, et al. eds. *Austalia's Italians*. Sydney: Allen & Unwin, 140-154.

INTERVIEW IN THREE PARTS

*The dialogue below includes parts of on-going conver-
sations with Frank Paci and consists of excerpts from
an interview which Dino Minni conducted in 1984,
parts of an interview with Joe Pivato from 1990 and
additional questions from 2001.*

Minni: Frank, you first wrote stories about North
American characters. What made you turn and
focus on Italian-Canadian families?

Frank: In 1972, twenty years after my family had
emigrated, I went back to Italy for my first trip. I
didn't realize it at the time, but this trip was the
catalyst that finally made me see that I had to
come to terms with my Italian background before
I could write about anything else. Before and after
the trip I had written five novels that no one
wanted to publish. The trip dramatically im-
pressed upon me the wide gulf between the Canadian and the Italian cultures and the depth of
my heritage, which I had been too naïve and
stupid to appreciate. The trip also made me appreciate my parents. For the first time I began to
see them clearly. Beforehand I had only seen
them in the context of Northern Ontario Canada,
if you know what I mean. Seeing them from the
Italian context completed the picture, so to speak.
When I started to write *The Italians* I had in the

back of my mind to celebrate my parents and
others like them, to thank them for what they had
done. This opened up a wealth of deep feeling
that I had never handled in other books.

Minni: Are you saying that you have a need to write
about your Italian-Canadian background, a sense
perhaps that things should not be lost ?

Paci: Yes, there is a need to preserve the accomplishments of my parents, with the accent on "serve."
I had the voice which they didn't have. It's this
very sense of preserving that acts as a catharsis,
because as you're writing the story of your parents you're also coming to terms with your background and defining yourself in an historical
context. Also, in the very act of writing fiction –
that is, in literally becoming the characters and
things you're writing about – you see real-life
people and things more as they are. This is the
humility I spoke about before – a humility that
produces compassion.

Minni: Writing, then, is a form of catharsis for you.
Was your childhood painful?

Paci: I didn't have a painful childhood, but I did have
a painful adolescence. My secure and contented
world came tumbling down because of certain
events that cut me off from everything that had
nurtured me. I wouldn't be surprised if most
writers have some sort of inner or outer wound
that spurs them to engage in such a lonely and

financially unrewarding a vocation as writing. Maybe this phrase from Hegel goes some way in explaining it: "The hand that inflicts the wound is also the hand that heals it." He was speaking of the wound caused by Adam's Fall. Also, of course, we all want to be loved and accepted in our own way.

Minni: In your novels the main characters all ask the same question. Who am I? Must Canadians look overseas for the answer, for their identity?

Paci: It goes without saying that Canadians of Italian descent should look overseas to get a more complete sense of their identities. Everyone is a historical creature and must look for his identity in the events that have shaped him. It's not only a question of identity. It's an ontological question.

Pivato: When did you first discover that you wanted to be a creative writer?

Paci: The answer to this is very complicated – I've sought to answer it in my novel, *Black Blood* (1991). A few facts suggest my writing inclinations. I became a voracious reader once I realized I wasn't as good an athlete as I thought I was. Or maybe the reading came first, which diminished by powers to see the balls and pucks clearly. There you have part of the complication. Another fact is that my father bought me a typewriter out of the blue when I was in high school. Another fact is that I reacted against my family and part of this reaction was the fact that my parents didn't read, had no books in the house, so, of course, that's precisely what I tried to correct in their lives. Another fact is that my safe secure world came crashing down on me when I was an adolescent, including my faith – and you can make a pretty good argument that writing is a form of mythologizing to compensate for the loss of the old myths. Also, there's the fact that the writer is someone out to cure himself of the terrible wound in his psyche, or to transform reality according to his incredible vanity, or to reinterpret the past to make some sense of the mystery of it all. I don't know. Another factor is my fascination with language, the power of language to transform people's lives and reality. But, probably, the most concrete reason was that it seemed the most ideal way of finding out who I was and what I was on earth for. These things built up slowly, but by second year in university when I wrote my first short story and carried it around in my back pocket, I seemed to jump from one level of being into another – and there I saw the path open for me. At the University of Toronto I later enrolled in Dave Godfrey's creative writing course and also met Margaret Laurence who encouraged my writing.

Pivato: English Canadian writing is dominated by the canonical writers of Ontario. Would you describe Italian-Canadian writing as a marginal literature?

Paci: Well, the very designation "Italian-Canadian" is a problem because by referring to a body of work as Italian-Canadian we are automatically ascribing marginality to it. That's our fault. And of course if some of these writers work in Italian, then they are automatically cutting off the mainstream reader. I don't think of myself as an Italian-Canadian writer. I'm simply a writer, who lives in Canada, uses English, and is of Italian descent. There's a big difference. I don't know, but does Joy Kogawa think of herself as a Japanese-Canadian writer? I doubt it. If you mean marginal in the sense that this body of work is not accepted as mainstream, then probably yes. But that's not the fault of the writers. It is rather the fault of readers, mostly those who aren't ready to concede their mainstream ethnic biases (i.e. British) to "marginal" ethnic cultures. There's an understandable fear here of displacement – and, of course, the mainstream ethnic culture has the grip on the channels of cultural power.

Pivato: Your own writing is outside the mainstream since it deals with marginal characters: immigrants, their children, immigrant women, a handicapped protagonist, Northern Ontario and other outsiders. Why are you interested in these non-heroic people?

Paci: The obvious answer is that this is where I come from. The interesting question is how such an oddity as a writer emerge from such soil? I disagree with you. Immigrants are not marginal in Canada, nor are women and children. The other three types, obviously don't describe the majority of people. And I wouldn't necessarily say that these people are non-heroic. For example, a man who works hard for his family in a factory can be much more heroic than a Mafia gangster who intimidates people according to the codes of the American West. Of course the latter will attract more readers. But that is the fault of the readers. The popular conception of heroism is not necessarily the right conception. I'm more interested in the quiet hero and heroine, someone who will make the right choice in the face of majority values. Most of your questions lead off into problems of value, questions of ethics, and problems of meaning. What is true heroism, for example? What kind of people do we look up to? Who should be the exemplars of our behaviour? These answers have to do with the age-old ethical, political, and religious questions of what it means to be a true human being. This is precisely what my work seeks to answer.

Pivato: I have found that ethnic minority writers are often focused on chronicling the immigrant experience and may become overly concerned with realism. Do you share this preoccupation?

Paci: How do you see "realism?" I see it as the narrator being more concerned with the object of narration than the consciousness observing the object. The writer certainly has to be concerned with the way the story and characters must best be rendered. The subject matter itself finds its best method, as Faulkner would say. This made him at times an "experimentalist," but only in the sense that he was passionately concerned with the subject matter. If someone experiments just to be "modern," he's barking up the wrong tree. If a new way of rendering character or consciousness comes, it comes. If it doesn't it doesn't. When you are dealing with the immigrant experience, you're sometimes dealing with simpler states on consciousness that have to be rendered in so-called realistic ways, which more properly should be called mimetic ways. Fiction, per se, is never real. It's always a fabrication of a different world, a mimetic world, in which all levels of consciousness have a place. The question is, rather, where is the line between fictional language and poetic language? I would put *Finnegans Wake* and *The Waves,* for example, in the poetic camp. In fiction there's a narrator and there's a story and the story happens to someone in a certain place. You can play all you want with those four basic elements, but I think you need the four of them, otherwise you don't have the re-creation of felt experience. If you have an author, for example, breaking into her story and exposing the story as a fabrication, then that's all part of the larger story: in other words it's just another way of creating verisimilitude with so-called reality. Every story tries to be "real" by being "unreal."

Pivato: How would you describe the evolution of your writing? (1990)

Paci: My writing is becoming more and more prayerful, more and more revelatory of a new kind of spirituality that has done with the old encrusted disciplines of institutionalized religion. If, in becoming prayerful, it becomes less fictional and less "artistic," whatever that means, then so be it. I don't believe that fiction or art in general is above everything, is its own god, I think that fiction and art "serve" a higher purpose in life. What that higher purpose is I don't exactly know yet. I have inklings, I have certain ideas, but until I've carried them out in some sort of communal action then they remain mere abstractions. Of course, the art of writing is a communal act. Except there are very few listeners out there. There are too many people who are lost in their blooming health, lost in their disgraceful lives. I guess my job from now on is to find out what there is to say that is worth saying and to find out what listeners there are to hear what is worth listening to.

Pivato: How would you describe the evolution of your writing? (2001)

Paci: First of all, I'm beginning to see more and more that it is not "my" writing. It is simply "the" writing. But for the purposes of communication in the conventional modes, I will refer to it as "mine." Due to the influence of Godfrey during my university years, the writing started as experimentalist. I was enamoured of the French *nouveau roman* and people like Joyce and Faulkner. But I didn't have enough command of language or a strong enough sense of identity back then to be very successful. Actually, I was too egotistical to know who I was. Four abortive novels were the result of this false start. However, I was learning through all the mistakes. After much frustration and pain, it occurred to me that I had to plunge into my own immigrant background and come to terms with it before I could do anything else as a writer. And in order to be faithful and honest to that background, and in order to make it readable to the very people it was honouring, I had to record it in a "realist" style. The first three published novels were the result of that phase. I remember, during that time, that I felt obligated in my own small way to render the immigrant experience of the ordinary and hardworking people who had made a new life for themselves, and to set them against the gangsters and other more flamboyant ethnic stereotypes which were getting all the exposure in the media.

Pivato: I have often noted that you and other novelists, Caterina Edwards, Nino Ricci and Marisa De Franceschi, have consciously written against the Godfather stereotypes. That is what is attractive

F.G. PACI
141

about Italian-Canadian writers, their uncompromising honesty.

Paci: Later I felt I had not been honest enough in these renditions, and the *Black Blood* series evolved from that. The series also sprang from a need to chart an inner journey, as it were, an inner journey of self-discovery towards the no-self. The *Black Blood* series is an ongoing project that will last a lifetime. The fifth novel in this series is *Italian Shoes*. The next novel, *Lisa James*, has already been written. Then I have jumped ahead in time and started to deal with Mark Trecroci's present circumstances –and the people who preoccupy his life. One such novel, *Losers* (which deals with students and teachers), is slated for publication in the fall of 2002. Two others are in the works-in-progress stage. My interests now tend to deal with what Mark calls "finding traces of the divine" in ordinary life and shedding all the illusions that make us so visibly stupid in life. In other words, to recognize what the great thinkers and prophets really said and did and try to live by their black blood and their example.

Pivato: In *Sex and Character* (1993) the setting is Rochdale College and Yorkville in the Toronto of the 1960s. What did you find interesting about this time and place?

Paci: Whatever I found interesting specifically is in the novel. But, in general and in hindsight, what interested me is the impermanence of everything. I was around Rochdale before, during and after. I saw the idealism and enthusiasm change into something quite sinister. During the sixties people were caught up in so many things – some noble, some ignoble – but the whole thing was swept away so easily, it seemed to me. For Yorkville, that was literally the case since it was changed into a trendy upscale place almost overnight. Just like the vibrancy of the Italian area in my hometown was sort of swept away. When this happens I tend to think that the only way to keep things permanent is to record them, to set them down. Because, of course, ideas and words – black blood – outlast most things.

Pivato: In *The Rooming-House* Mark Trecroci is trying to become a writer after surviving the 1960s. He seems to have left his Italian family far behind in the Soo and abandoned his ethnic culture. Is this a necessary step in order for Mark to become a writer?

Paci: Yes, Mark needs that radical break from his family and his background before he can ever achieve a sense of self (that is not egotistical) and definitely before he can achieve that perspective necessary to write about anything. Of course, he was trying to gain that perspective internally while he was with his family. He was filling himself with black blood. But he needed to do that in a physical way as well –away from family.

He also, in a way, has to detach himself from all human beings in general, to go through the gauntlet, as it were, to achieve the insight necessary to be a recorder of people's consciousness.

Pivato: The latest volume of the *Black Blood* series is *Italian Shoes* in which Mark Trecroci returns to Italy for the first time. This pilgrimage in many ethnic minority novels has been romanticized. Why have you treated this trip in such a plain style?

Paci: Well, you call these narratives ethnic novels. I certainly don't see *Italian Shoes* as an ethnic novel. As for romanticism, I don't believe in it. It's false in perpetuating too many self-delusions, even in its more lofty versions in the Romantic poets (though I don't dismiss all their notions). To be honest to one's characters, and to eliminate delusions as well as illusions, one must be scrupulously honest in rendering them as they are. Therefore, the style of writing should not draw attention to itself. I'm not saying I'm entirely successful in this, but I try to be.

Pivato: With *Icelands* (1999) you moved away from the *Black Blood* series of novels to focus on our Canadian obsession with hockey. Why did you do this?

Paci: I was personally involved with the "Canadian obsession with hockey" with my own son for ten years. I grew up in Sault Ste. Marie, which is still a hotbed of hockey. The obsession with sports in general is a world-wide phenomenon of the twentieth century. Why are we so obsessed with sports? With playing sports and watching sports? Is it because we're obsessed with competition, with getting the better of someone else? Is it because it's a vicarious way of satisfying our instincts for power? Is it a means of "intensifying the moment," in contrast to our everyday humdrum lives? Or is it a form of purgation for the masses, much as the ancient Greek tragedy was? Whatever the case, hockey is supposed to be our national pastime. It's what we are supposed to be the best at. So I wanted to show what that dream presently involves in the day-to-day lives of ordinary people.

Pivato: One final remark. With *Losers* (2002) you explore religious subjects which you have visited in past novels. It will be interesting to see if you return to these themes again and in greater detail and depth. Maybe we will let your new novels address these questions.

BRIEF BIOGRAPHY

Pesaro is a city on the Adriatic coast of the Marche region of north central Italy.

In 1948, Franco Gilberto Paci, whose parents lived in a village outside the city, was born in Pesaro – in a landscape of poor agricultural villages and rolling hills topped by the occasional ruined castle. The young Paci emigrated to Canada with his parents in 1952 and grew up in the immigrant west end of Sault Ste. Marie, Ontario. He attended St. Mary's College, a Catholic high school run by the Basilian Fathers who often appear in his novels. To attend university he migrated south to Toronto and enrolled in St. Michael's College, a Basilian affiliated institution at the University of Toronto. To pay his university expenses he spent the summers working in the steel plant back in the Sault. His education includes a B.A. in English (1970) and B.Ed. (1975) from the U. of T. where he was encouraged to write by Margaret Laurence who was Writer-in-Residence at the time. There he also met Dave Godfrey, Marian Engel and other Canadian writers.

His first novel, *The Italians,* appeared in 1978 and was one of the first novels to deal with the Italian-Canadian immigrant experience. In 1980 he earned an M.A. in English from Carleton University in Ottawa. His second novel, *Black Madonna* (1982), is still his most popular book because of the depiction of immigrant women and feminist ideas. Paci is one of the most important Italian-Canadian novelist working in English and helped to create the phenomenon of Italian-Canadian literature. He writes in the realist tradition and explores the struggles of Italian immigrant families in Northern Ontario. The philosophical dimensions of personal identity are evident in *Black Madonna* and in *The Father* (1984). In October 1983 Paci was invited to Edmonton, Alberta, to give a reading with local writer, Henry Kreisel. In May 1984 he was invited to Rome for the first conference on Italian-Canadian writing and history. In 1988-89 he was the first writer to hold the Mariano Elia Chair in Italian-Canadian Studies at York University, Toronto.

In 1991 Paci began a narrative series with *Black Blood*, followed with *Under the Bridge* (1992), and *Sex and Character* (1993), which recreates a scene between the protagonist, an aspiring writer, and Margaret Laurence. This *Bildungsroman* series includes *The Rooming-House* (1996) and *Italian Shoes* (2002). He departed from the *Black Blood* series in 1999 and brought out *Icelands*, which deals with the triumphs and pitfalls of families and hockey. In many of Paci's novels the characters from northern Ontario are struggling with life in Toronto, and so he explores migration and exile within Canada. Another novel, *Losers* (2002), deals with religious themes which he plans to develop in other novels. Short stories and excerpts from novels by F.G. Paci have been included in *Other Solitudes* (1990), *Pens of Many Colours* (1993), *Making a Difference* (1996), and *The Anthol-*

ogy of Italian-Canadian Writing (1998). Frank Paci is married, with a son, and teaches high school in Mississauga, Ontario.

SELECTED BIBLIOGRAPHY

NOVELS

The Italians. Ottawa: Oberon Press, 1978. New American Library, 1980.

Black Madonna. Ottawa: Oberon Press, 1982.

The Father. Ottawa: Oberon Press, 1984.

La Famille Gaetano. Trans. *The Italians* by Robert Paquin. Montreal: Guernica, 1990.

Black Blood. Ottawa: Oberon Press, 1991.

Under the Bridge. Ottawa: Oberon Press, 1992.

Sex and Character. Ottawa: Oberon Press, 1993.

The Rooming-House. Ottawa: Oberon Press, 1996.

Icelands. Ottawa: Oberon Press, 1999.

Italian Shoes. Toronto: Guernica Editions, 2002.

Losers. Ottawa: Oberon Press, 2002.

SHORT STORIES

"Chapter 12" in *Italian Canadian Voices.* ed. Caroline Morgan Di Giovanni. Oakville: Mosaic Press. 1984.

"The Stone Garden," in *Other Solitudes: Canadian Multicultural Fictions.* Eds. Linda Hutcheon & Marion Richmond. Toronto: Oxford U. P., 1990.

"Mancuso's and Sons," in *Pens of Many Colours: A Canadian Reader.* Eds. Eva Karpinski & Ian Lea. Toronto: Harcourt Brace Jovanovich Canada, 1993.

"From Black Madonna," in *Making a Difference: Canadian Multicultural Literature.* Ed. Smaro Kamboureli. Toronto: Oxford U. P., 1996.

"Growing Up with the Movies," in *The Anthology of Italian-Canadian Writing.* ed. J. Pivato. Toronto: Guernica Editions, 1998.

"In Italy," *The Toronto Review of Contemporary Writing Abroad.* 16, 3 (1998).

"One eye filled with night," *The Canadian Forum* Vol. LI, 609 (October, 1971) 32-37.

ESSAYS AND INTERVIEWS

"Tasks of the Canadian Novelist Writing on Immigrant Themes," in *Contrasts: Comparative Essays on Italian-Canadian Writing.* ed. J. Pivato. Montreal: Guernica Editions, 1985.

"An Interview with Frank Paci," by C.D. Minni. *Canadian Literature* 106 (1985).

"Interview with F.G. Paci," by J. Pivato in *Other Solitudes.* Op. cit.

ESSAYS ON F.G. PACI

Bonanno, Giovanni. "The Search for Identity: An Analysis of Frank Paci's Novels," in *Canada: The verbal Creation.* ed. Alfredo Rizzardi. Abano Terme: Piovan Ed. 1985.

Morgan Di Giovanni, Caroline. "The Image of Women in Italian Canadian Writing," *Italian Canadiana*, 11 (1995).

Pivato, Joseph. "Hating the Self: John Marlyn and Frank Paci," in *Echo: Essays on Other Literatures.* Toronto: Guernica Editions, 1994.

Sciff Zamaro, Roberta. "Black Madonna: A search for the Great Mother," in *Contrasts: Comparative Essays on Italian-Canadian Writing.* Montreal: Guernica, 1985 and 1990.

Tuzi, Marino. "Provisionality, Multiplicity, and the Ironies of Identity in *Black Madonna*" in *The Power of Allegiances.* Toronto: Guernica, 1997.

Waxman, Martin. "The Discipline of Discovery," *Books in Canada* XXIII, 8 (Nov. 1994).

Letters in *A Very Large Soul: Selected Letters from Margaret Laurence to Canadian Writers.* ed. J. A. Wainwright. Toronto: 1995.

THESES

Canton, Licia. *The Question of Identity in Italian-Canadian Fiction.* Ph.D. Études Anglaises, Université de Montréal, 1998.

Tuzi, Marino. *Identity, Multiplicity and Representational Strategies in Italian-Canadian Fiction.* Ph.D. English Literature. York University, Toronto. 1995.

LIST OF CONTRIBUTORS

Anna Carlevaris is an art historian who lives and works in Montreal where she teaches at Concordia University and Dawson College. Her research areas include immigrant identity in contemporary art, photography, and Canadian Art. Recent writings include catalogue essays in *Le Mois de la Photo à Montréal* and *Light Festival of Photography* Winnipeg; as well as essays in *Visio*, *Poliester*, *History of Photography* and *C Magazine*. She is also an independent art curator.

Caterina Edwards is an Alberta novelist who has taught creative writing at the University of Alberta, Grant MacEwan College and Athabasca University. Her books include: *The Lion's Mouth*, *Homeground* (a play), *A Whiter Shade of Pale/ Becoming Emma*, and *The Island of the Nightingales* (2000), which won the Howard O'Hagan award for short fiction.

C.D. Minni was a Vancouver writer, editor and reviewer who published *Other Selves* (1985), edited *Ricordi: Things Remembered* (1989) and co-edited with Anna Foschi, *Writers in Transition* (1990). Dino Minni died of MS in 1989.

Enoch Padolsky teaches English at Carleton University in Ottawa. He has co-edited *Migration and the Transformation of Cultures* (1992) and has published essay on ethnic minority writing in *Canadian Ethnic Studies*, *The Journal of Canadian Studies*, *The International Journal of Canadian Studies* and many other publications.

Joseph Pivato teaches Comparative Literature at Athabasca University. His books include: *Echo: Essays on Other Literatures*, *Contrasts: Comparative Essays on Italian-Canadian Writing*, *Caterina Edwards: Essays on Her Works* and *The Anthology of Italian-Canadian Writing*, all with Guernica Editions.

Gaetano Rando teaches Italian and English Language Studies at the University of Wollongong in Australia. His books include: *Language and Cultural Identity* (1990), *La barracata dell'Eureka: Una sommossa democratica in Australia* (2000) and *Australia's Italians* (1992), which he co-edited.

Roberta Sciff Zamaro earned an M.A. at the University of Alberta with a thesis on F.G. Paci and now teaches English in Gorizia, Italy.

Marino Tuzi earned his Ph.D. at York University with a thesis on Italian-Canadian literature and now teaches Canadian Studies at Seneca College in Toronto. He has published *The Power of Allegiances: Identity, Culture and Representational Strategies* (Guernica, 1997) and several articles on ethnic minority writing.